MANAGING
HUMAN PRODUCTIVITY

MANAGING
HUMAN PRODUCTIVITY
People Are Your
Best Investment

Stephen J. Holoviak and
Susan Stone Sipkoff

New York
Westport, Connecticut
London

Library of Congress Cataloging-in-Publication Data

Holoviak, Stephen J.
  Managing human productivity.

  Bibliography: p.
  Includes index.
  1. Personnel management—United States.
2. Manpower planning—United States. 3. Human
capital—United States. I. Sipkoff, Susan Stone.
II. Title.
HF5549.2.U5H65   1987   658.3'14   86-25247
ISBN 0-275-92481-5 (alk. paper)

Library of Congress Catalog Card Number: 86-25247
ISBN: 0-275-92481-5

First published in 1987

Praeger Publishers, 521 Fifth Avenue, New York, NY 10175
A division of Greenwood Press, Inc.

Printed in the United States of America

∞™

The paper used in this book complies with the Permanent Paper Standard issued by the National Information Standards Organization
(Z39.48-1984).

10 9 8 7 6 5 4 3 2 1

Contents

List of Figures and Tables

FIGURES

TABLES

Acknowledgments

Writing this book has been a community project—a study in people working harmoniously and enthusiastically toward a common goal. As a microcosm of the workplace, the work process itself has provided great insight into how people are motivated and kept productive and enthusiastic, even under high pressure and stress. It speaks well for the potential of workers in our society.

In that this has been a community project, many people made substantial contributions to the work. Our special thanks and heartfelt appreciation go to Dr. David A. DeCenzo for his contributions to the work, which were enormous. Dr. Paula Kirby of Sperry Corporation, Sharon Holoviak, Professional Counselor, James A. Walker, Professional Historian for the U.S. Army, and Dr. Myron Gable also made significant contributions, which were greatly appreciated.

Also very important in helping us to understand the realities of employer/employee relations from the point of view of the practitioner were: Michael S. Bailey, Manager of Labor Relations for Hershey Chocolate Company; Dr. Anthony F. Ceddia, President of Shippensburg University; Art Conrad, Vice President for Employee Relations for the Chambersburg Hospital; Gerald J. Kirschke, Manager of Employee and Community Relations for Capital Products Corporation; and Martin B. Skane, Personnel and Plant Services Manager for CertainFeed Corporation. Thank you all for your time and invaluable insights into what is happening in the field.

We wish to thank Karen Craig, our typist, for her thoughtful and expert typing of our often less than legible work. We would also like to thank Dr. Joseph Hunt, Dean of the College of Business of Shippensburg University for his support in the project. And, finally, we would like to thank our families for their support, insights, and understanding during this process.

Although it is a little unusual, we would also like to thank each other. Our partnership is one to which we bring very different perspectives, backgrounds, approaches, skills and ways of working. These differences have led to a very stimulating, creative, and productive working environment. We are mutually appreciative of this interaction and its results.

I HUMAN PRODUCTIVITY

Part I sets the base upon which to build our knowledge of how to enhance our investment in people to the mutual benefit of both the organization and the employee. Chapter 1 introduces the reader to an innovative concept of managing people even as other important investments are managed. Chapter 2 provides a background as to why as managers we are often faced with an atmosphere of mistrust and adversarial feelings. Chapter 3 goes into the foundations of personnel/human resource management and shows how they may be fitted to our concept. the state of the art in employee/employer relations is applied to assure us a solid foundation before we move into a discussion of the new-wave ideas of human resource management.

1   Invest In People?

"Employees don't depreciate. Their value to the organization, when they are well-maintained, only appreciates."
— David Decenzo

INTRODUCTION

Throughout recorded history people have written about their visions of what the future may hold. One need only look at the Book of Revelations and the writings of Nostradamus for examples. In a slightly different fashion, people have written about their visions of what could be. Political figures frequently receive attention for that type of activity. The Great Society of Lyndon Johnson is an example in recent history of a political vision combined with a proactive movement that to some degree successfully realized it.

The history of the United States is short compared to that of other nations. A great deal, however, has been accomplished in that short time. We have gone from literally clearing trees for roads, factories, schools, and other necessities of civilization to building one of the most sophisticated societies in the world.

When people try to identify the reason for the poor record of treating workers in the United States they often point to this whirlwind of activity. We did not ease into an industrial revolution. Many activities and events provided simultaneous input into how things were done, many of which receive more

3

detailed and documented explanations in Chapter 2. Briefly, there were

1) rapid input of cheap labor via immigration;
2) beginnings of the industrial revolution;
3) availability of free or cheap land;
4) labor mobility to acquire the land;
5) the need to provide services to a large number of new citizens;
6) the recent birth of the nation and its laws;
7) regular involvement in domestic and international conflict; and
8) economic theories that did not separate the worker from other factors of production.

Management theorists believe that under the conditions implied by the items on the above list, an autocratic business management style may well have been the most efficient. In none of the literature published are strong claims made that participative management might have been expedient.

The problem now appears to be that there have been significant changes since the whirlwind days of our early beginnings:

1) In recent years we have been trying to limit immigration. There is not the need for mass influx of people to settle vacant land, and immigration now contributes to the social welfare state dilemma.
2) The nation is not functioning in the humble beginnings of the industrial revolution. In fact, the shift to a service-oriented economy has occurred.
3) Land is no longer a cheap commodity.
4) Labor mobility problems are a well-documented phenomena.
5) Our laws now have a significant level of case history and the United States is the oldest democracy in the world.
6) The frequency of international conflict may have slowed, but the spending to prepare for the events has not.
7) New economic philosophies are presenting the individual as an important economic factor.

Current personnel/labor relations philosophers, academics, and practitioners looking at the changes in the scenario are recording new visions of what could be. They are calling for changes in how organizations treat employees, and demanding that the "happenstance" way these resources are treated be changed.

It took an oil embargo to bring about the changes in the conservation of oil; polluted waters to change our perspective there; and the bleak reality that the United States is no longer the number one industrial power to begin to bring changes in how human resources are handled.

The path to change is not destined to be without difficulty. Former attitudes are not easily changed, but the tools for change are present. In many cases we could simply adapt our thinking regarding machinery and apply it to people.

Managers all over the world are making capital investment decisions. They are, for the most part, taking great care and putting a lot of thought and time into gathering detailed information regarding their alternative purchasing possibilities. Consider equipment purchasing in a production situation. Managers are considering which machine is going to be able to do the job required and be the most durable. They are, after all, considering investing thousands, even tens of thousands, or even millions of dollars in the machine, and the decision has to be the right one.

Once the machine is purchased, great care will be taken to maintain the investment that has been made. Not only has a good bit of money been sunk into the machine, but its smooth functioning is crucial to the organization's meeting its objectives. Without a machine in good repair, production goals will not be met. Replacement is costly, time-consuming, and may involve down time due to the necessity of retraining people with respect to how to use a new piece of equipment.

Do managers understand the nature of their investments in people? Do managers understand that, when someone is hired, that, too, is an investment? If an organization hires a mid-level executive for $30,000, taking into account inflation for raises and the like, the average organization will spend $875,000 in salary, $207,000 in average benefits, and $87,000 in tax-free or tax-favored benefits over 20 years.

In the case of a machine purchase, people tend to be committed to maintenance of that machine, understanding the potential costs to the company of down time and the potential revenues that result from productive time. They know the costs of replacement and retraining and realize that proper maintenance and repair capabilities will help maximize the profitability of their investment. They do not tend to consider heavy capital investments as disposable properties. Neither would a manager ever conceive of purchasing a piece of computer equipment at a cost of $200,000 and abusing it. If the life expectancy of that computer is ten years, excluding opportunity cost and the like that's a $20,000 per year investment—the same investment we might be making in an employee.

An employee's down time costs the company plenty in terms of lost productivity; and replacement and retraining are also expensive and time-consuming. The techniques of caring for employee investments properly is the subject of this book. When these techniques are followed, the rate of return will match or exceed anything possible with machines.

DIRECTIONS FOR CHANGE

Background Conditions

The problem for many managers is what direction to take in positive treatment of employees. Many managers are well schooled in the finance and economics of management. But few are equally trained in human resource management. For most who have received some training in management, it has proven to be mostly a history lesson. That is, we were taught that if we "did something" to employees, like changing a light bulb, they would respond positively. The emphasis did not even have to be positive and productivity would increase. We learned of the "Hawthorne Effect" and, unfortunately, paternalization of the employee was the lesson we took away with us from the training.

In this book we want to take the reader beyond paternalization and into the techniques of proactive management, which has strong positive effects. We are not interested in manipulative actions designed only to keep people on the job, rather we are interested in a style of labor/management interaction that can lead to a partnership for organization growth.

Economic conditions have highlighted the importance of understanding the utilization of all resources — specifically, what they cost and what they return. One measure of return is productivity. Harvard's D. Quinn Mills was quoted in the January 30, 1986 BNA Bulletin as recently reflecting that

> Managers justify proposed capital investments by citing the number of jobs they will eliminate. . . . These attitudes remain very deeply ingrained in much of our management and employee workforce and are a major factor in limiting the contribution which labor-management relations can make to productivity improvement. It is important that economic reasoning be the catalyst for positive growth. Not the reason to point a finger of blame.

An example of economic data that can serve as a reason for cooperation is the change in wage rates and productivity relative to principal trading nations of the United States. These figures have been alarming to both labor and management. Statistics indicate that the productivity of United States' principal trading partners is increasing at a greater rate than that of the United States. Returns to companies on their investments in people have tended to be low.

Clearly, this has been a source of concern for all involved and informed managers today are taking steps to understand the nature of their investments better and to protect their investments, including those in people. In fact, amazing as it may sound, we are beginning to realize that our real returns, our real chances for competitive advantage and profitability may actually come through our investments in people.

Investment in people needs to be viewed in the broad sense. The time spent in meaningful dialogue that reduces adversarial positioning of labor and management is an investment. Training our supervisors how to handle compliments properly, how to listen to employees, how to evaluate their progress, and how to interact with them on the job are topics discussed in Parts II and III; these are investments in people. And these are investments that will yield positive returns to management.

People are an important factor in the production process. Yet, we have treated this investment as an incidental asset. We have spent money on research and development required to increase the efficiency of machines and very little money on updating skills to increase the efficiency of our people.

Modern organizations are complex entities that must combine resources effectively to achieve their goals. The impact of foreign competition and domestic economic conditions have forced a rethinking of past strategies for achieving stated goals. A reality of this era has been the reevaluating of the role of workers as a pivotal resource at our disposal. How efficiently organizations utilize this resource may determine survival in the current competitive environment.

U.S. personnel and labor relations are in a state of transition. This transition challenges many of our basic policies, practices, and approaches in relation to managing human resources. The terms "labor relations" and "personnel" are too narrow and misleading for the current state of the field of managing people. As such, the approach of this book is also to focus on the transition and guide the reader into the new era of human resource management. The practical work of selling the program to upper management, unions, and other parties involved is the focus of Chapter 13.

Catalysts for Change

Conversations with practitioners through focus group interviews and survey research revealed that informed managers realize that their attitudes toward people need to be as positive and possess the same level of excitement and commitment as those toward new capital investments. They are beginning to understand that this will lead to higher levels of productivity—higher returns on their investments.

One major catalyst of the change in how management viewed personnel/labor relations began with the 1964 Civil Rights Act (Title VII–Equal Employment Opportunity) and the 1972 amendments to Title VII. It also began with Supreme Court decisions that complained that many of our employment selection devices and tests had a disparate effect on minorities and were not job-related. The beginning was the Occupational Health and Safety Act (OSHA); affirmative action law suits springing forth from a line of presidential executive orders; a more active National Labor Relations Board; and a host of other pieces of legislation discussed at greater length in Chapter 11.

A second major catalyst for change was the decline in worker output that began around 1969 and for the most part continues even now. There are, of course, examples of industries and companies where this trend was not present, but for the country as a whole, output fell. When this decline was coupled with the inflation that was present in the early 1980s, some serious conditions began to exist in U.S. industries.

A third catalyst was the emergence of foreign competition. Many so-called second- and third-world countries recovered from wars and were reaping the benefits of their economic development programs. Programs included building quality products at competitive prices. Managerial development programs were carried out without direct U.S. involvement. In the case of Japan and a few others, personnel utilized managerial concepts rejected by U.S. companies. Only when faced with the success of the techniques did quality circles and quality of work life become noticed by U.S. executives.

A fourth catalyst involved a work force that was different from the earlier ones in various ways. This new work force is better educated and demands more satisfaction from a job than only a paycheck. It desires creative input to the product and more control over its working destiny. They are less willing to tolerate autocratic managerial styles, and appear to resent the poor management practices that allowed their companies to end up in their current conditions.

A fifth catalyst is finally taking form in the early 1980s. It involves some profound changes in managerial style and the realization that people are an asset to the organization. There were examples of individual companies seeing this back in the late 1950s, but they are the exception.

To handle the numerous changes, companies revamped their personnel departments so that by the late 1970s they had stopped being career graveyards and began to be looked upon as springboards to upper management. The expertise of the personnel director was necessary to keep the organization from getting into trouble. For many organizations their evolutionary pattern stopped with the legal and social mandates of the 1960s and 1970s. While an improvement, there still remains a quantum leap before companies can reach enlightened managerial stages.

CONFUSION IN THE PROCESS

Those who observed the era from 1964 to 1982 were certainly entertained by the actions of our managers. The list of fad solutions to our problems were everywhere. They ranged from MBO (management by objectives) Theory Z and the Sixty Second Manager and lists of various incentive systems to T-Groups and Qualitative Management. As discussed in Chapter 3, the 1980s saw the realization that training could produce positive results for organizations. Unfortunately, not all the suppliers of the programs are equally skilled, and many are overpaid for the level of content. Many organizations failed to present an orderly progression of training leading to some common body of knowledge to be possessed by the attendees when the programs were complete.

It is no wonder that when quality circles and participative management, the focus of Chapter 4, emerged on the scene, skepticism was readily apparent. Union and nonunion employees were confident this was just another fad approach that would pass given sufficient time. Middle-level managers had a vision of more work and reduced authority. Upper-level managers, not committed to the concept, accepted the program as a big suggestion system or an add-on device that would not upset anything else. They did not accept the fact of a complete change in managerial style accompanying quality circles and participative management.

With the whirlwind of activity happening around the person in charge of people handling, it is easier to understand the frantic changes in titles and the grasping at fads that appeared to be solutions. The environment is not what could be considered calm. It is doubtful a calm environment will occur in the near future. What has helped is a maturity of professionals in the field, more appropriate training from the academic environment, and time to sort out the impact of all the legal and social changes.

THE MOVEMENT TO HUMAN RESOURCES

When organizations come to grips with the reality of what they are facing in a contemporary environment, the move to become human resource managers becomes a possibility. Among various possibilities are the following: 1) decentralization of decision making to the lowest possible point, 2) enhanced mutuality of interest to reduce adversarial tension, 3) the presence of quality circles or some form of participative management and quality of work life program, 4) information sharing between parties, and 5) attention to employees' needs for growth and for physical and emotional health.

The goal is to balance coverage of traditionally used policies, practices, and approaches with the emerging concerns of practitioners, scholars, and students in the field. Traditional areas are discussed in light of new research findings that have helped to focus our attention upon this area. These research findings suggest that past methods may not help organizations operate in an efficient manner in reaching their goals. Emerging concepts offered are not fads or quick fixes. Rather they are tools that will help us to handle the job of human resources management. While there is a continuing emphasis on improving the work environment for employees and increasing organization productivity, these emerging concepts help in achieving these goals more efficiently.

The first section of the book contains the basics for understanding what is happening in terms of human productivity, including: this first chapter, which introduces the framework and tone for what follows; a chapter presenting the history of management and its people; and a chapter on traditional foundations for managing people. Reasons are suggested to explain why contemporary workers still feel the need to join unions.

In Part II the authors address current challenges and identify approaches for handling them, including discussions of quality circles, stress, and counseling.

Part III contains a practical look at collective bargaining, including factors that influence negotiations, how to collect necessary data, how to cost out labor contracts, and how to write formal agreements in clear language, thus facilitating more effective administration of formal agreements between management and labor. It also contains information regarding corrective action and formal arbitration. Issues such as discipline, grievance handling, and arbitration are considered in such a way that readers should be able to resolve issues at the first-line supervisor level. These concepts must still be addressed. We still have to go to the bargaining table. Hopefully, though, these concepts have been presented in such a way that the mind-set of those involved in negotiations will not be that of adversaries in battle, but rather of trained professionals doing their jobs.

Part IV talks about internal marketing and future trends as related to people in the work force. The need to recruit good people and maintain them through caring about them, counseling them, including them, working with them, and giving them avenues for growth is paramount. Through doing this the company not only protects its investment in this valuable resource, but also substantially increases its chances for success in the marketplace through the resultant reduction in turnover rates and increases in morale and productivity, and, hence, profitability.

Do we expect resistance from employees to the techniques suggested in this book? Research on the topic suggests the employee will not be an obstacle to change. From popular newsstand psychology magazines to in-depth research in academic and professional journals, we read that workers' attitudes have changed. They want more from life than just a job. Both sexes want more control over their working destiny and appear to favor enlightened treatment by organizations. For instance, males may want to be involved in child-rearing activities and females want equal access to jobs yet wish to retain flexibility in handling family responsibilities.

Can we assume the fact that individual workers are accepting changes automatically means that unions will endorse new ideas? As one would expect, change within organizations comes about quite slowly. Yet, as discussed in Chapter 4, unions are demonstrating support for participative management. In Chapters 5, 6, 8, and 9 we see entry of the unions into support for positive human relations and professional negotiating techniques that will smooth the way for enhanced productivity by their members.

The chapters that follow give an overview of where we have been, where we are, and where we are going. The reader will observe that, while many of the functions remain largely the same, new perspectives have been applied resulting in substantially different approaches. The hope is that these approaches will yield substantially different results, including more realistic and profitable costs for and returns on business people's investments in people.

2 History: We've Come A Long Way

INTRODUCTION

The history of the labor movement in the United States has reflected the struggle of labor to become an equal partner with management in business. On one hand labor has attempted to gain economic security through the contribution of skills. On the other hand those who control the production of goods and services have also attempted to gain economic security by making a profit from their efforts. In order to realize that profit they were required to control the cost of their product or service, a significant portion of which has always been labor. Unfortunately, management traditionally perceived labor as just one more cost to control, without realizing the nature of these very valuable human resources.

LABOR EQUALITY AND THE REVOLUTIONARY WAR

The desire of labor for equality and an adversarial relationship with business began before the American Revolution. In order to combat a labor shortage in colonial America, business interests enacted regulations that ensured wages were homogeneous and curtailed movement between the trades. When workers solicited wages above the going rate, they were fined (Foner 1976). In addition, business people were paying low wages. A 1769 colonial businessman defended the payment of low wages: "It is certain that high wages more frequently make laboring people miserable; they too commonly employ their spare time and cash in debauching their morals and ruining their health." (Foner 1976)

Fundamental differences between labor and the more established elements of society extended into the political arena as well. The desire of some colonists to influence politics led to the formation of organizations by skilled laborers, such as the Sons of Liberty and The Committee of Mechanics. Criticism was levied against the political views of these groups and their position in society.

> These sheep, simple as they are, can not be pulled as heretofore. In short, there is no ruling them; . . . While they correspond with other colonies, call and dismiss popular assemblies, make resolves to bind the conscience of the rest of mankind, bully poor printers, and exert with full force all other tribunal powers it is impossible to curb them. (Foner 1976)

The adversarial relationship between business and labor continued with the formation of the new government. Despite the participation of the Committee of Mechanics in the Revolutionary War, its members did not gain a position of equality under the new government. After the Revolution, the Committee of Mechanics complained that "The Committee of Merchants did refuse the mechanics a representation in their body, or to consult with their committee or offer their names of the persons nominated to them for concurrence." (Foner 1976)

THE CONSPIRACY ERA

Workers organized themselves into trade groups in Philadelphia, New York, and Boston. The early trade union movement concerns were welfare activities, higher wages, minimum piece rates, shorter hours, enforcement of apprenticeship regulations, and exclusive union hiring. In 1786 the Philadelphia printers launched the first authenticated strike (Gitlow 1963). The bootmakers and shoemakers went on strike in Philadelphia in 1799. Although this strike led to the first recorded meeting between workers and employer representatives, it also resulted in a conspiracy charge against the bootmakers and shoemakers. The verdict against the shoemakers read:

> Not being content to work at the usual rates, but continuing unjustly and oppressively to increase the rates [they] did conspire, confederate, and unlawfully agree together that they would not work but at certain large rates to the damage, injury, and prejudice of the masters employing them and of the

citizens of the commonwealth generally, and to the great damage of other journeymen, to the evil example of others, and against the peace and dignity of the Commonwealth of Pennsylvania. (Maher 1965)

Some historians have concluded the conspiracy trials occurred because labor's drive for higher wages ran counter to a creed in America that justified almost anything in support of unbridled growth in the country following the Revolutionary War (Maher 1965). While that may be true, the verdict also reflected the same attitude that prevailed among the business community before the Revolutionary War. Labor's drive for higher wages was counter not only to the creed supporting unbridled growth in the country but also to the creed supporting higher profits for business.

The conspiracy trial verdict moved labor action to the political arena. Between 1820 and 1830, labor candidates were elected to the Philadelphia City Council and the Pennsylvania State Legislature. Over 50 local unions were active in Philadelphia and New York City. Their common interest was the promotion of shorter work hours and union made goods (Gitlow 1963).

The United States economy experienced a series of ups and downs with respective increases and decreases in union membership. Simultaneously, the industrial revolution contributed to a rise in non-craft jobs. There was a new wave of immigration, especially English miners. Familiar with the political activities of 1840 England, the miners formed some of the first labor unions in the Pennsylvania anthracite coal regions (American Federation of Labor 1930).

THE KNIGHTS OF LABOR

Although there were several labor organizations functioning by 1886, the largest was the Knights of Labor. The Knights of Labor, a national organization, claimed 700,000 members. This membership was organized into a national body or general assembly that exercised control over numerous district assemblies. The Knights of Labor program called for an eight-hour day, equal pay for equal work by women, the abolition of child labor, public ownership of utilities, and the establishment of cooperatives. The Knights of Labor attempted to accomplish its goals through educational and political methods rather than collective bargaining. Strikes were to be employed only as a last resort (Gitlow 1963).

The Knights of Labor, craft unions, and the socialist movement attempted to gain recognition of labor as an equal partner in United States business. To be sure, labor experimented with many methods to gain equality. Terrence Powderly, an early leader of the Knights of Labor, was accused of inconsistency in the methods he used to accomplish labor's goals. Powderly agreed and said he could change his mind and tactics as often as he pleased in order to accomplish the goals of the Knights (Dick 1972).

The attitude of the industrialists, however, was unchanged from the pre-Revolutionary War period. Industrialist Frederich Townsend Martin captured the overall attitude when he said:

> We are the rich; we own America; we got it; God knows how, but we intend to keep it if we can by throwing all tremendous weight of our support, our influence, our money, our political connections, our hungry congressmen, our public-speaking demagogues into the scale against any legislature, any political platform, and presidential campaign that threatens our estate. (Beaty 1980)

The theories of social Darwinism, survival of the fittest, were espoused to give scientific credence to the Martin attitude. John D. Rockefeller, in his Sunday School address, stated:

> The growth of a large business is merely a survival of the fittest. . . . The American Beauty Rose can be produced in the splendor and fragrance which bring cheer to its beholder only by sacrificing the early buds that grow up around it. This is not an evil tendency in business. It is merely the working out of a law of nature and a law of God. (Hogstadter 1959)

IMMIGRANTS IN THE LABOR MOVEMENT

The wave of immigration continued and more immigrants experienced with the labor movement in Europe arrived. The European labor experience was expressed through political means and the new immigrants pushed for use of the same methods within the United States. Their political opinions espoused a class consciousness expressed in statements such as: "The bosses care nothing for your nationality except to divide you and neither should you so that you may unite" (Kraditor 1981).

The immigrants were not the only element of American society that found the extreme wealth of the major industrialists repugnant. Many Americans disapproved of these individuals.

Horrible conditions in the mines and factories that employed more and more workers were in conflict with the traditional image of the independent American. There was also a lack of rules and norms within big industry. Industrialists showed little concern for cruel and amoral employees. They lived in lavish and aristocratic settings that included buying titled sons-in-law for their daughters (Kraditor 1981). John Stepp of the U.S. Department of Labor notes one foundation of adversarial labor/management relationship as having developed through the use of shop foremen. In 1890 there were 90,000 foremen in the U.S. By 1900 there were 360,000, which represents a 400 percent increase in ten years. These foremen exercised unrestricted authority over their subordinates.

The management style that emerged from this milieu often was that style described via the Theory X prototype presented by McGregor. In reviewing the assumptions underlying certain X-type management behavior, McGregor hypothesized that workers chose to be directed, had little ambition, and did not want responsibility. Managers assumed that getting labor to put forth effort on behalf of the organization required a threatening or coercive management style.

EARLY STRIKE VIOLENCE

Disparity of standards between labor and management and harsh working conditions led to violent strikes by labor. On September 23, 1913, 900 miners struck a coalfield in southern Colorado. The coalfield managers blamed the strike on radical agitators. The animosity of management to labor was obvious in management's position:

> When men such as these together with cheap college professors and still cheaper writers in the muck raking magazines, supplemented by a lot of milk and water preachers with little or no religion and less common sense are permitted to assault the businessmen who have built up great industries and have done more to make this country what it is than all the other groups combined, it is time for rigorous measures to be taken to stop these vicious teachings which are being sown throughout the country. (Jaffe 1972)

On October 17, 1913, a gun battle erupted at the mine between the strikers and the sheriffs. Eleven children and two women were found dead the following day. They had suffocated in the bottom of a cave where they had hidden to escape the gunfire. The incident became known as the Ludlow Massacre (Jaffe 1972).

EARLY HISTORY OF THE FAILURE TO INVEST IN PEOPLE

The crux of the issue underlying the labor movement was expressed in a dissenting legal opinion in the court case of Vegelahn versus Gutner in 1896:

> One of the eternal conflicts out of which life is made up is that effort of every man to get the most he can for his services, and that of society, disguised under the name of capital, to get his services for the least possible return. Combination on the one side is patient and powerful. Combination on the other is the necessary and desirable counterpart if the battle is to be carried on in a fair and equal way. (Gregory 1958)

The opinion in the Vegelahn case recognized the struggle between investments in capital equipment and investments in the employee, in which the cost of labor was seen by management as a direct threat to the amount of profit a company could make.

While industrialists and management were united in their approach to unions, organized labor was divided and equally condemning of those whom it would not admit into its ranks. The International Workers of the World (IWW) declared that every local union should ensure that the "slum" element, "the degenerates, the drunks and those men who are so far gone they have lost all manhood, are kept away from the halls and meeting places of the IWW" (Kraditor 1981).

EMERGENCE OF THE AMERICAN FEDERATION OF LABOR

Out of the maelstrom of divergent viewpoints and movements, the trade unionists, in particular the American Federation of Labor (AFL), emerged as the voice of labor. Although the AFL offered no ideological challenge to capitalism, it sought immediate relief for the worker through a gain in purchasing power. Samuel Gompers, the AFL leader, believed that "only the concrete and the immediate were material" (Diggins 1973). Looked upon as the bane of the left, Gompers constantly campaigned for the worker to be recognized as an equal: "I maintain that the working people are in too great a need of immediate improvements in their conditions to allow them to forego them in the endeavour to deviate their energies to an idealistic end, however beautiful to complete." (Gompers 1957)

Influence of the Socialists

Gompers, representing the majority viewpoint of the AFL, and the socialist faction of the AFL, particularly the IWW, battled over the proper objectives of the labor movement. The IWW charged that the AFL was not the labor movement, but rather a small percentage of the working class. Moreover, the socialists claimed neither the minority, who would overthrow capitalism, nor the majority, who were attached to any union at all (Kraditor 1981). Gompers countered by saying he was falsely charged with trying to drive the socialists out of the movement and that they were being intolerant of others' opinions. Gompers claimed his only condition was that, regardless of what political party he belonged to, a man should be able to maintain a good standing membership in a trade union (Gompers 1957).

Aileen S. Kraditor has pointed out, in *The Radical Persuasion,* that it was difficult for workers to decide what theories and programs were socialist, which were labor's and, in some cases, even which were capitalists' (Kraditor 1981). In the final analysis, no matter whether labor was organized as a trade union or a socialist party, the desire was to achieve recognition for its contribution. Gompers, in a speech in Logansport, Indiana, on February 11, 1891, echoed the desires of all individuals who sold their labor: "You can not weigh a human soul on the same scales with a piece of pork. You can not weigh the heart and soul of a child with the same scales upon which you weigh any other commodity." (Gompers 1957)

Influence of World War I on the AFL

World War I was used by Gompers as another opportunity to legitimize the labor movement and make it part of the system. In fact, according to some, Gompers used his involvement in the war movement to destroy dual unions and the socialist movement. In 1912 the socialists were staging a resurgence. The socialist candidate for presidency of the AFL received 5,073 votes to Gompers's 11,974. Gompers's active involvement of the AFL in the Allied cause in World War I, to which the socialists were opposed, made the socialists objects of criticism and cost them support in the union election (Larson 1975). The AFL also received support from leading financiers and major industries. Gompers blamed "German inspiration" for the 1915 strikes in the munitions plants. The union leader, anxious to prove the commitment of the AFL to the war cause, petitioned Ralph Eastley of the National Civic Federation to launch an investigation of the strike. Eastley agreed with Gompers and went to Henry P. Davidson of the J. P. Morgan trusts, who assessed each manufacturer $2,500 to help pay for the investigation of the strikes in the munitions plants (Larson 1975).

Industry, however, was not impacted in the same manner as labor. One United States senator charged that industry "held a gun to Uncle Sam's head." The president of McKinney Steele said that "he was making more money out of the war than the average human ought to" (Larson 1975). Thus, after World War I labor experienced the same frustrations it did after the Revolutionary War. Their "preferred status" was gone since the government no longer needed to please the labor leaders. Worse, labor failed during the war years to strengthen its membership and prepare for leaner times (Larson 1975).

The years between World War I and World War II were ones of confusion. By 1919 the purchasing power of the dollar had shrunk and there were 3,600 strikes (Jaffe 1972).

The industrialists wanted to go back to the way things were before the war despite the Clayton and Adamson Acts. Employers called the open shop the American Way and the labor movement was blamed for the Red Scare (Jaffe 1972). The Red Scare reached such proportions of hysteria that a sailor shot a man to death in Washington, D.C., for failing to rise for the National Anthem; and in Hammond, Indiana, a jury took two minutes to acquit a man who had murdered an alien for saying, "to hell with the United States" (Jaffe 1972). The Red Scare, followed by the Great Depression, led to a further decline of union membership and activity.

THE NEED FOR LEGISLATION

It was not until the New Deal and the National Recovery Act (NRA) of June 16, 1933, that unions began to regain lost ground. The NRA authorized $3.3 billion to stimulate the economy and provided self-regulation through industrial codes. The codes helped end destructive competition, raise wages, and spread employment by limiting hours of labor. Section 7a of the act, which guaranteed labor the right to organize and be free from interference, was particularly important. Moreover, no employee or person seeking employment was required to join any company union, and employers had to comply with minimum hours of labor and rates of pay (Cronon 1963).

The NRA stimulated a renewed interest in labor unions. However, despite the gain of 1.5 million new members, the AFL was badly divided over whether or not to organize workers in mass production industries. Management's stand was not divided. According to General Hugh Johnson, the NRA administrator, "Management fought for every ounce of benefit from the act." For example, the automotive industry cajoled the NRA to approve a clause in a bill to permit hiring and firing on the basis of individual merit. Labor charged that the merit clause was being used to get rid of active union members (Cronon 1963). The courts became involved in the issue as well. They assured the unions they had the privilege to organize and employers had the right to campaign against employee organization. Judge Learned Hand stated in his *The National Labor Relations Board (NLRB)* v. *Nederbush* in 1941, opinion: "What to an outsider will be no more than the vigorous presentation of a conviction, to an employee may be the manifestation of a determination which is not safe to thwart." (Gregory 1958)

Despite the role of the courts and government, the adversarial relationship between business and labor continued. When the nation entered World War II, the War Department discovered that the problem with the Wagner Act (the National Labor Relations Act of 1935) was not the unions, but rather "what to do about contractors who refused to comply with the Wagner Act" (Fairchild and Grossman 1959). In July 1937 the Comptroller General of the United States ruled that the NLRB and the courts were responsible for enforcing the Wagner Act. Several major companies, including Ford Motor Company, failed to comply. On October 2, 1940, the NLRB concluded that a Wagner Act violation on the part of an employer was still binding and conclusive until overturned by the courts. In reality, a firm violating the Wagner Act could still be awarded a war department contract (Fairchild and Grossman 1959).

One victory does not win a war. Bethlehem Steel Corporation refused to accept contracts that required compliance with the Wagner Act. Bethlehem's refusal along with refusals of other companies led to the revocation of Procurement Circular 43 on June 5, 1941 (Fairchild and Grossman 1959).

Despite a pledge by labor, there were strikes during the war years. The soaring cost of living and accumulated strains had more effect on the rank and file than the warnings of public officials or even labor leaders. This resulted in a series of plant seizures by the federal government, as well as probationary legislation and morale campaigns, all of which contributed to the prevention of strikes and maintained war production (Fairchild and Grossman 1959).

FIRST ATTEMPTS AT LABOR PARTICIPATION IN DECISION MAKING

Since colonial times, labor has attempted to become an equal partner with its employers. Labor experimented with craft unions, socialism, and progressivism until the leadership of Samuel Gompers set labor upon its present course—trade unionism. Trade unionism made labor a partner in industry. Unfortunately, the partnership, because of its adversarial nature, remained an unequal one. Labor found itself in the position of a person who is responsible for balancing a checkbook without having the authority to determine how much is in the account.

To be sure, labor made strides in its attempt to secure a more equitable partnership. Labor arbitration, first begun in 1799, is now a routine part of the labor process. According to Dean Shulman, arbitration is an integral part of the system of self-government, designed to aid management in its quest for efficiency and to assist union leadership in its participation in the enterprise (Hays 1966).

Labor participation on federal government boards in World War I was another milestone. In 1962, when the government sought to avert inflation through wage and price guidelines, labor arbitration was no longer confined to typical labor and management issues (Wellington 1968).

Labor has, in some cases, cooperated with its employers on some issues. For example, instead of fighting to break up the coal trusts, labor has fought for their consolidation. This occurred because electric power companies now have the ability to switch from coal to gas and because of this are able to exert and enforce their demands on the coal industry. In this situation, labor and management became equal partners in an effort to satisfy a customer.

Unfortunately, the coal industry experience is the exception. The adversarial relationship between labor and management is still present. Labor still lacks an effective role in the decision-making process. The Clayton Act, signed on October 15, 1914, declared that the labor of a human being was not a commodity or article of commerce. Unfortunately, the need to understand and comply with the Clayton Act has remained largely unmet (Gregory 1958).

PARTICIPATION IN QUALITY CIRCLES

It is important to note that when examining the history of labor/management cooperation there is the same abundance of information available as for the history of labor/management conflict. Labor and management have moved over time away from authoritarianism toward participation in their relationship for this change in philosophy. Theory X behaviors emanating from the early 1900s, such as Frederick Taylor's Scientific Management, have not always moved into Theory Y behaviors or team-oriented Theory Z orientations. Although there have been gradual shifts in focus that have allowed us to design our work environments using new insights, the roots of any current cooperation between management and labor, such as quality circle programs, when examined, show developments in team-building and participative management as far back as World War I. Like many ideas that pass the test of time, the essential concept remains intact while the application or execution changes to reflect the economy, the market, or the specific work environment.

The idea of increasing employee participation in the workplace was not invented in Japan as is commonly thought, nor were the process methodologies of group problem solving and on-the-job decision making. The ideas started in the United States. During World War I, American industry's first formal and planned experiences with worker and management problem-solving teams began. At this time, approximately 100 large businesses formed "shop committees" that had the express objective of setting the terms and conditions of workers' employment. Although some of the shop committees of the 1920s were mandated by the government, many companies established these worker-management groups on their own. Kodak, Goodyear Tire and Rubber, Standard Oil, Proctor and Gamble, and Youngstown Steel formed teams to coordinate activities that would enhance cooperation and production; adjust grievances and complaints; and review wages, work load, and other terms of employment affecting the work force. The teams linked much of their activity to improving shop efficiency and the economies related to production. In a 1920 report, a Bridgeport Brass executive endorsed the shop committee on his site: "During the last two years, 328 suggestions for economies and improvements in manufacturing equipment and methods have been submitted, of which 28 percent have been adopted by management."

Over the 17-year life span of the Baltimore and Ohio Railroad Shop Committee Program, over 32,000 suggestions of work area improvements were generated. Eighty-six percent of these suggestions were approved by management and implemented in the workplace. Some goal change areas identified by the shop committees at the railroad include

1) modifying management attitudes;
2) recruiting the cooperation of foremen;
3) solving hygiene problems;
4) gaining management support;
5) recognizing employee ability and initiative;
6) increasing communication between employees and management; and
7) identifying talent.

The innovations practiced by the shop committees fell out of style for some time, but the undercurrent remained as an energizer for the movement of "Multiple Management," which is resurfacing as today's participative management trend. "Multiple Management" can be defined as a plan in which a team of employees meets regularly to determine, analyze, and resolve work-related problems. This system was effective in reducing communication gaps among various levels of management. It sought to bring about greater pride in the workplace and also enhance worker involvement. McCormick and Company of Baltimore, Maryland, first adopted multiple management boards during the 1930s. These boards included:

1) The Junior Board (suggested ideas for improvements in packaging, sales, and products).
2) The Sales Board (suggestions to help product sales).
3) The Factory Board (sought to increase productivity).

It was determined at that time that the success of a multiple management system was highly dependent on the enthusiastic support of middle management, which was thought to feel threatened by such an approach.

During the 1940s there was a nationwide campaign spearheaded to mobilize both the material and human resources required for the war effort. The War Production Board was organized as a central agency that would help various labor committees establish themselves throughout production facilities across the country. The theme of such activities was to increase war production, improve employee morale, and ensure good working relationships between management and labor. Labor leaders from various unions endorsed the management-labor committees, numbering some 5,000 in all from plant to plant. About 1,000 of these committees, or 20 percent, were considered notable successes for contributions they made to improving productivity and raising the morale in facilities where they operated. Examples of their problem-solving successes as submitted to the production board are as follows:

1) During the first few months of the program, $47 million was saved through civilian employees' suggestions alone.
2) More than $25 million had been saved in man-hours and materials in ship construction through the U.S. Maritime Commission suggestion system.
3) In one year alone, civilian employees saved the Navy $30 million, as reported by the Incentive Division.

THE CHANGE FROM ADVERSARIAL ATTITUDES BEGINS

Previous management behavior styles differ radically from present management trends evidenced in the workplace. *The Harvard Business Review* (Ewing 1981) conducted a survey of businesspeople's attitudes that revealed a clear trend toward less autocratic practices and a growing support on the part of executives for enlarging the influence of employees. In addition, organizations have been employing an increasingly larger number of programs that rely on and promote labor/management relations. In the 1984 *IAQC Conference Report: State of the Art Forum on Quantity and Improvement,* a behavioral survey of American and Japanese managers reported interesting findings. When asked if they heeded advice from subordinates, 63 percent of the American managers surveyed said they did to a considerable extent. (This figure is compared to 53.5 percent of the Japanese managers surveyed.) Such notations in labor/management history clearly depict a departure from the authoritarian standards used at the start of our industrial age.

Labor exercised a great influence as unions became generally acceptable, as bargaining structures stabilized, and as compensation packages adjusted to the cost of living. By the 1970s, however, the United States started to experience stiff foreign competition. Certain industries became deregulated and the boom and expansion of the high-technology industries caused shifts in traditional industrial patterns. Many traditional union industries became nonunion. Union avoidance became the practice of many industries. Standard compensation criteria gave way to a system based on productivity and the ability to pay. Employee stock options programs and gainsharing became popular. Recent longitudinal studies of worker attitudes show evidence of a trend toward a greater interest in intrinsic rewards, including that of added responsibility in the workplace (Casey 1979).

Mroczkowski (1984) outlines data collected over the last few years showing organizations employing programs that rely on and promote cooperative labor-management relations:

1) Between 1976 and 1978, the number of employees affected by labor-management committees rose by over 40 percent.
2) Between 1978 and 1982, the number of organizations using Quality of Working Life programs doubled.
3) The use of profit sharing has risen sharply recently, and in early 1983, about 17 million U.S. workers were covered by profit-sharing plans.

These emerging trends underline a central conceptual theme, that of participative management. Its important role in today's workplace cannot be disregarded.

The New York Stock Exchange study on "People and Productivity" (1982) reported the acknowledgement of a change in management philosophy, especially among the larger corporations. Throughout the study, participative management through the development of human resource programs was charted among U.S. corporations by the Exchange's Business Research Division. Findings included:

1) In companies with human resource programs, typically 60 percent of the employees are involved in some facet of the program, some 13 million workers in all. This 13 million accounts for less than one-third of the 41 million people currently employed in corporations with one hundred or more employees.
2) Companies report that their efforts are successful in:
   - increasing productivity
   - raising morale
   - reducing costs
   - improving service
   - raising product quality
   - reducing employee turnover, absenteeism, lateness, and grievances

3) Management considers participative management a significant long-run approach to raising productivity and not a passing fad.

4) Quality circles are spreading, particularly among manufacturing firms and large companies: two-thirds of companies with 5,000 or more employees include them in their personnel or human resources programs.

SUMMARY

After a very difficult two-hundred-year growth period, labor and management seem to be on the road to recognizing their need for each other.

Various pieces of legislation helped force the issue of cooperation. But it has rested for the most part at that point, i.e., a legislated cooperation. This chapter has offered several theories why the adversarial arrangement between labor and management persists. The positive side is that after two hundred years of domestic conflict change is occurring.

Quality circles and labor representation on boards of directors are certainly steps in the right direction. Labor must look upon management as an essential partner in the industrial process. Labor must be viewed by management as an equal partner in finding the "solution" in today's competitive business environment, not as part of the problem.

3 Foundations of Human Resource Management

INTRODUCTION

The field of human resource management has changed from a function that handled vacation schedules and company outings to one that has a fully integrated perspective. The roles, responsibilities, and accountabilities of the human resource function have gained vital importance. Whatever the perspective of human resources, however, fundamental activities are conducted. It is on these fundamental activities—hiring, paying, and training people—that we focus in this chapter. The complexities of today's human resource function cannot be handled effectively by a one chapter overview. It would require an entire textbook, at the least. However, those central issues that comprise any human resource function can be addressed.

The foundation of any human resource management effort lies in analyzing jobs. Because of the importance of this activity, and its subsequent use in other areas, the discussion of traditional human resources will begin with an overview of the job analysis process. Following the job analysis discussion, compensation activities in human resources will be considered, including compensation philosophies and benefits being offered. With the compensation function serving as a skeletal base, the remaining areas will be considered as they logically fit within the human resource management function. First, people must be hired—a process that will be explored from its inception. Then, people must be trained. Training and its ancillary services will be considered. Finally, discussion will focus on the myriad of activities offered to maintain a positive work environment. These activities will be grouped under the umbrella of employee relations.

JOB ANALYSIS

Job analysis serves as the foundation for all activities in the human resource function. Job analysis as an activity provides a detailed representation of what skills, knowledge, and abilities are needed to perform successfully any given job in an organization. Accordingly, job analysis serves as the impetus for recruiting, for pay structures, and for Equal Employment Opportunity considerations.

Conducting a job analysis serves, then, as good business sense. Before determining whom to hire and what to pay a particular position, the requirements of the job must be understood clearly. It is these requirements that provide a sketch of the individual needed for the job. If a candidate has the requirements, then the candidate is qualified. Using this information, an organization is hiring based on job-related requirements. This, again, is a business necessity. It is also through these same requirements that we determine the relative worth of each job. Without this relative worth, an organization may be paying too much for a position, or paying too little. The ramifications of these actions lead to a reduction in an organization's bottom line. To avoid this potential disaster, an analysis of the jobs in the organization must be conducted. The next section looks specifically at the process of job analysis and its main by-products—the job descriptions.

The Process of Job Analysis

There are as many possibilities for conducting a job analysis as one can imagine. A review of various textbooks, journal articles, or research on the topic verifies that no theorists can agree on one best method. About the only conclusion that can be drawn is that a combination of practices must be used to ensure that all the information regarding a job has been captured. But how does one go about the process itself?

The most popular means of conducting a job analysis is the questionnaire method. The questionnaire method of job analysis involves sending a prepared set of questions to incumbents and asking each to complete it regarding how each one sees the job. The questionnaire is usually constructed using an open-ended question format, asking each incumbent about skills, requirements of the job, special certifications needed, number of people supervised, and reporting relationships. The questionnaire can provide a significant amount of information, but is sometimes inaccurate or written in a manner that is difficult to understand.

The observation method of job analysis is also used. This method is a throwback to the early 1900s, when the scientific management approach was prevalent. The scientific management approach attempted to find the "one best way" of doing a job. In many instances, this meant spending a great deal of time watching, recording, and timing the activities of the workers. The observation method is similar, yet the concept of the "stop watch" observer is removed. However, the observation method implies just that, watching workers work, recording their activities, and writing about what was seen. Using this type of methodology can be very effective, provided that enough time is spent to see all aspects of the job accurately and the observer is skilled enough to pick up the intricacies of the job. Even when these two assumptions are true, this is a costly method.

Another popular method is the interview method. The interview method of job analysis revolves around the one-on-one dialogue between the job analyst and the worker. Usually a structured format is used by the analyst in an effort to gain as much relevant information as possible about the job. While the interview method is effective, important aspects of the job may be missed simply because the incumbent has forgotten an activity or trivialized others.

The supervisory method of job analysis, on the other hand, revolves around the premise that supervisors are quite knowledgeable about the jobs they supervise. Again, in many cases, this method can capture good information, but may also miss important elements of a job because the supervisor cannot have the most complete knowledge of every job supervised. This could cause a misrepresentation of the job being analyzed.

These are the four most mentioned techniques or methodologies employed in conducting a job analysis. Each method has its benefits, and each benefit has its cost. No one method, by itself, can result in an effective job analysis. What is needed then is a process that incorporates a number of these methods, capitalizing on the benefits each has to offer.

An Effective Approach to Analyzing Jobs

Before embarking on a job analysis project, it is important to lay out a plan of action. Haphazard job analysis is of little use to the organization; yet, even haphazard efforts are better than no efforts. Assume, however, that an organization embarking on a job analysis project has decided what jobs to analyze, who is going to do the analysis, and how the information is to be kept and used after the process is over. With that in mind, consider the following process, which is built on capturing the best available information, participation, and communications.

The first step involves informing line management what will be done. In this step, your role, how the job analysis is to be conducted, their role, and the time frames are explained. This step is without a doubt the most vital step in the entire process. Without commitment from line managers to the project, it is doomed to failure. Many line areas see this activity as a waste of their time, something that may affect their workers' productivity, and also something that "only" those in personnel need. Again, explaining the purpose, and the importance of the job analysis, its impact on productivity and the organization as a whole, can eliminate much of the discussion around analyzing jobs. After the initial meeting, the process begins formally.

Incumbents in jobs to be analyzed are sent questionnaires to complete. These questionnaires are designed to capture the information needed to analyze the job accurately. More specifically, the questionnaire assesses the basic reason the job exists, work performed on both a routine and non-routine basis, what skills an incumbent needs to perform successfully on the job, the financial responsibility of the incumbent, the number of people the incumbent supervises, and leaves an open space for the incumbent to provide any information the questionnaire may have missed. This provides information from one source, the job holder. Additional steps may enhance the process.

Once the job holder has completed the questionnaire, it should be given to the supervisor for review. Here the supervisor can augment the information, increase its accuracy, and add anything that may have been missed. Using this step increases the chances of obtaining the most accurate information available.

After the supervisor's review, the questionnaire is signed and returned to the analyst. The analyst then writes the first draft of the job description and makes an appointment to interview the incumbent and the supervisor. During this interview, the analyst clarifies any information that may have been vague or department-specific, verifies the content, and gathers any additional information that may have come to light after the questionnaire and its subsequent review were completed.

The analyst now has all the information available and must construct the second draft of the job description. Depending on the information gained in the interview, the first and second draft of the job description may be identical. Nonetheless, once the second draft is complete, it is sent back to the line manager for approval. The interesting point here is line management approval. If the line manager will not approve the draft, reasons are ascertained in writing and corrections or changes are made in the job description draft. This cycle continues until approval is gained. As a point of reference, expect at least two refinements before approval is obtained.

JOB DESCRIPTIONS

Consider the by-product of the job analysis: the job description. The job description is a written portrayal of a given job at the point in time the job was analyzed. It gives the reader a complete representation of the activities involved in the job, its place in the organization, and the people and fiduciary responsibilities associated with the job. The purpose of such a portrayal is to give an accurate picture of the job and to identify the skills needed by an incumbent to perform this job.

The job description will also serve as the tool for many other activities in human resource management. Specifically, it will be evaluated so that a wage may be assigned to the job. What is evaluated? Generally the skills, knowledge, responsibilities, and problem-solving abilities required are evaluated. The more skills required, the more responsibility one has, the more impact a solution to a problem has, the more one is generally paid. Thus, the big difference in the chief executive officer's pay and that of a bookkeeper in the accounting department is due to differences in skills, responsibilities, and problem-solving ability.

The job description will also be used in the recruiting process. If the skills and knowledge are known, the recruiting effort becomes one of matching candidates' abilities to the job. Again, and not to belabor the point, this is a sound business activity, one devoid of discrimination—because nowhere in the skills requirement does race, creed, color, sex, age or national origin enter into the picture.

Because of the importance of the job description and its subsequent implications, it is hard to imagine that any organization would not conduct a job analysis. It is important that the job descriptions be current. A job description two years or older should be suspect due to the question of whether or not the information is still accurate. In fact, from a hiring perspective, an employment representative hiring based on information from an outdated job description is more likely to hire a candidate whose qualifications will not accurately match the requirements of the job. This is a disservice to the candidate and to the organization.

COMPENSATION AND BENEFITS

Pay Structures

Besides being generally responsible for conducting job analyses, human resources also is responsible for setting the pay structure of the organization and administering employee benefits.

Before any salary structure is developed by an organization, it must be philosophically based and supported by top management. There are so many factors that go into setting salary structure that time and space preclude identifying all of them, even if this feat were possible. Aside from state and federal laws mandating certain wage levels, the philosophy of a fair wage implies that companies compensate workers based on their worth to the organization. Keep in mind the earlier statement that job descriptions are used in determining a job's worth. Thus, job descriptions serve only as the means of determining relative worth of each job within the wage structure accepted by the organization.

A compensation system built around a fair wage involves many factors: labor market, source of candidates, and specialized skills required. Traditionally, compensation departments embark on salary-planning endeavors. These endeavors usually result in identifying average salary levels for similar jobs in other organizations. Generally, each major department in an organization has some type of professional affiliation that can provide salary information. For example, the American Society for Personnel Administration (ASPA) collects salary information on personnel professionals. Anyone interested in establishing a wage for an employment specialist can obtain a reasonable figure through ASPA. This can be repeated for almost every specialty.

Source of candidates and specialized skills required must also be considered. If skills are rare, or if national recruitment is needed, the salary structure may have to be altered. Internal pay equity must also be ensured, or else talented individuals will soon realize they are worth more in the marketplace, which increases turnover. Each organization must decide how much it is going to pay, and because of that, structuring a salary framework becomes a company-specific activity.

Benefits

Benefits were first provided to employees to "sweeten the pot." As a recruiting device, benefits were a means of attracting good candidates while simultaneously reducing the direct-wage bill. However, as time has progressed and workers have become more attuned to their total compensation package, offering various benefits to employees has become a major organizational activity. Coupled with this new perspective is the fact that benefits now add approximately 45 cents on the dollar to the wage bill. In other words, your $20,000-a-year salaried employee costs you $29,000—$20,000 in direct salary and $9,000 in fringe benefits. These fringes are expected. There is no short-cut means of reducing fringe benefit costs. The issue is how to manage benefits more efficiently—a major problem in many of today's organizations.

The work force prior to the late 1960s had a much different impact on organizations. During this early period, the work force was characterized as middle-aged, family-oriented, blue-collar male employees, individuals working for a single company throughout their entire work life (Sutcliff and Schuster 1985). For these individuals, the benefits they expected were in line with a long-term company commitment. This commitment represented a need for employer-funded retirement programs; medical coverage; life insurance policies; and vacation, holiday, and sick leaves (Sutcliff and Schuster 1985). Because these were fairly common benefit programs, costs were reasonable and could be passed on to the customers in the form of a product price increase without much notice. This period was the heyday for benefit administrators.

However, the turbulent 1970s brought major revisions in benefit offerings. The work force became more mobile, more educated, and more demanding of benefits that suited their needs. Long-term commitment to an organization was waning. The younger employees sought more say in what benefits they received. The influx of women into the labor force also triggered a major change in benefit offerings.

Benefits were now being seen more as a means of enhancing an employee's quality of work life. More health coverage was expected by the younger workers, and less emphasis was placed on longer term offerings, e.g., retirement (Sutcliff and Schuster 1985). Costs, too, soared and the new creature created to tackle the problem was cost containment. Employers looked at cafeteria offerings as a way to reduce costs, while at the same time providing an opportunity to offer benefits that were more targeted to the individual employee. Thus, a young single employee might choose the benefit of time off from work, while a married employee with a family might choose more medical coverage. The concept of the cafeteria benefit plan is simple: there is only so much money that can be spent on employee benefits, so give the employee what he/she wants and maximize the impact of the offering. Unfortunately, the administrative nightmares involved in operating a cafeteria benefit plan soon took their toll and the cafeteria plans fell into disuse.

While cafeteria plans proved not to be the panacea for soaring benefit costs, they did indicate that employees are different and have different needs and expectations. Occurrences in the 1980s reinforced the view that organizations are not infallible, that some would not survive. This survival issue raised many concerns, for if the company did not survive, even the most efficient benefit program would become defunct. Employers, employees, and the general public began to review what companies could offer and still remain competitive. Newspapers in the early 1980s were replete with headline stories regarding wage concessions or givebacks. This was especially true in the unionized sector. Most of those givebacks came from employee fringe benefits. Again, the rising costs of fringe benefits; the younger more educated, mobile employee; and the international competitive nature of business all mandated reducing or containing fringe benefit costs.

Benefits in the Future

Certainly trying to predict what fringe benefits will look like by the year 2000 would be futile. However, there is a major movement in the area that is expected to continue. First of all, the issue of containing the costs of fringe benefits will continue. The main target is to contain health care costs—the largest expenditure, percentagewise, of fringe benefits. Federal and state governments, in conjunction with businesses and health insurers, are actively exploring ways to contain these costs. To date, we have seen an increase in health maintenance organizations (HMOs), which require employees to use specific facilities, specific doctors, and specific hospitals, all in an effort to obtain a fixed cost in providing health care. There is also an increase in preferred provider organizations (PPOs). PPOs are similar to HMOs, except that these providers agree to accept a fixed lower payment for services rendered in return for being identified as a preferred provider and sent additional clientele. Again, the health care arrangements are too complicated and too vast to cover effectively in this section. Suffice it to say that one can expect more drastic changes occurring in this field by the year 2000.

There are also more changes in how retirement programs are structured. Next to health insurance, retirement program funding is the most expensive. Again, the responsibility for retirement income is resting increasingly with the employees. While traditional retirement plans may continue in some form, many organizations are going to contributory plans—that is 401Ks, profit-sharing plans, and individual retirement accounts. Congress, so far, has been supportive of contributory retirement plan legislation and, based on the uncertainty surrounding the Social Security system, more legislation is expected.

Finally, probably the biggest change that will occur will be the reduction of merit pay increases. Because productivity improvements are needed for the U.S. as a whole to remain competitive, pay increases will be tied more to performance. This may mean that "pay progression will slow and more employees will not receive an increase every year" (Sutcliff and Schuster 1985). The impact of this fact is sure to be a dramatic one.

RECRUITMENT

While the recruitment function in human resources is not as intricate as the compensation and benefits area, it is equally important. Recruitment finds viable candidates, ensures that staffing levels are maintained, and is without a doubt the part of the organization most exposed to the public, all of which suggest that exploring the function is warranted. The following overview keys in on three areas: human resource planning, locating candidates, and interviewing.

Human Resource Planning

In its simplest form, human resource planning is the process of ensuring that current positions and projected positions are staffed. To conduct such a process requires an in-depth analysis of the organization, identifying the current skills possessed by all employees. These skills are stored in some capacity within the organization's human inventory. The current skills base is then compared to the strategic plan of the organization. If in the next five years the organization expects to be in a certain line of business, then staffing the personnel needs to accommodate entering that line of business is necessary. This process boils down then to matching the demand for a particular type of labor with the supply of that labor—both internal and external.

While there are many sophisticated human resource planning processes, they are seldom used. With the exception of extremely large corporations, few organizations operate a formal or informal human resource planning effort. This seems to be the result of the lack of long-term strategic planning. As a result, recruiters operate in a reactive fashion, usually having to fill more positions than possible in the time frame given. In some organizations, just keeping pace with filling turnover slots is a full-time endeavor. Hopefully, as organizations begin to plan more effectively in general, they will also begin to plan more effectively in this area. Until that time, human resource planning is primarily confined to textbook discussions.

Locating Candidate Sources

One of the greatest abilities a recruiter can have is the ability to locate viable candidates quickly. Advertising in the wrong location or using the wrong media results in lost time and may result in vacant positions and lost productivity. How the recruiter proceeds depends on the job, the time given to fill the position, the level of the job in the organization, and the type of recruiting budget available. It also depends on equal employment opportunity criteria and affirmative action concerns in the organization. This is quite a balancing act for the recruiter. Keeping the concept of job analysis in mind, hiring based on skills and ability to do the job will by-pass much of the Equal Employment Opportunity concerns. This is not to make light of EEO, but puts it in perspective. If the hiring criteria are job-related (validity) and used consistently (reliability), the possibility of a discriminatory charge is significantly reduced. But to be certain, a routine check of who has been hired can be helpful. If, even on the skill-based selection criteria, only white males are hired, selection criteria should be reviewed in order to avert future difficulties.

To maximize the recruiting dollar spent, recruiters must locate candidates effectively. Some of the more useful means of finding candidates are as follows:

1) *Newspaper Advertisement.* Placing an ad in the local newspaper, usually on Sunday in the employment section, is probably the quickest means of communication and the one that receives the most coverage. Newspaper ads are excellent for entry- and lower-level jobs in an organization. The average cost for a two-column ad is about $350, but the audience you reach is the intended audience. Newspaper ads are good if you want to examine many resumés. Remember, under EEO regulations, if a resumé is received, one must respond to the applicant who has applied, even if the response is one of no interest on the part of your organization. If many resumés are expected, use a blind box ad. The blind box ad eliminates the responsibility to respond—but it may also eliminate the resumé from the best candidates, because many job seekers are leery of sending a resumé to an unknown organization.

2) *Employee Referrals.* Employee referrals are excellent ways to locate possible candidates. This is built on the premise that good workers will refer good candidates—that no one would jeopardize a reputation by referring a known poor employee. Employee referrals are a good source for all positions, although rarely used at the very top of the organization. Nonetheless, it is quick and usually has positive results for the organization. One drawback is that employee referrals can breed nepotism or foster discrimination. Safeguards must be implemented to protect against such occurrences.

3) *Unsolicited Resumés.* Unsolicited resumes are another source of good applicants. Unfortunately, this process gets bogged down. Many more applications come in than job openings available. While unsolicited resumés and applications are good sources for lower-level jobs, processing these may become an administrative headache. As with newspaper ads, you must respond to the unsolicited applicant. This takes time and money and, for the most part, is not cost-effective to an organization.

4) *Professional Associations.* Earlier in this chapter, when referring to wage structures, we said most professions represented in

an organization have associations. These associations are good sources of candidates. Good candidates can be found either by attending a meeting and "networking" or by advertising in the association's publication. This method is excellent for professional positions, middle- to upper-level management positions, and for senior executives.

5) *Agencies.* Private employment agencies act as the recruiter for their client organizations. Sometimes referred to as "headhunters," these agencies locate candidates based on organizational requirements. Thus, all the "leg work" is removed and the recruiter is presented with two or three viable candidates. Agencies are growing in popularity. Because of their contacts, they can locate prospective employees more efficiently. They are usually locating candidates in higher levels of management for an organization, and for the most part are successful. The major drawback to using an agency may be the cost. Agencies usually earn a commission equal to 30 percent of the first year's salary. Thus, if an agency locates an upper-level manager in computer programming and the salary to that person is $80,000, the agency commission fee charged would be about $24,000. The company has benefited from a national search, and has paid for it. A national search may or may not be cost-effective, depending on the circumstances, including how much an in-house search would be and how much it would cost.

Interviewing

Many different avenues are available to screen applicants, such as weighted application forms, employment tests, and physical examinations. None is more widely used, or more often abused, than the interview. Research has indicated a plethora of reasons why interviews are unreliable and invalid. Nevertheless, the fact still remains that few, if any, individuals get into an organization without first having had some face-to-face contact with a hiring manager. It is important to describe the reasons underlying the negatives surrounding interviews.

The single, most problematic issue surrounding poor interviews is poor interviewers. Managers from all parts of the organization assume they are experts in candidate interviewing. Many assume that interviewing is something that comes naturally, that anyone can do it on a moment's notice. Nothing could be further from the truth.

First of all, effective interviewing requires skill. There should be a method or structure to the interview process. This, as research has shown, is seldom true of interviewing situations. The lack of a structure is the biggest contributing factor to poor interviewer performance. Unfortunately, like strategic planning, setting a plan of action for the interview takes more of an informal approach, if it is done at all. Without a plan, each candidate is likely to be dealt with differently. How, then, can a decision be made as to who is best suited for the position? A coin toss might be equally effective in identifying the best candidate.

Interviewer bias also affects interviewer performance. Human beings carry certain prejudices. These, unfortunately, can play havoc in an interview. For example, interviewers have a tendency to put too much emphasis on appearance. Candidates should have their best foot forward. If they show up sloppily dressed, the interviewer might interpret this as an indication of the candidate's commitment. This may be true in some situations, but not all. The individual's appearance should carry major weight only if it is related to job performance. The appearance of a candidate for a sales position or the position of president is very important. Requirements for the floor sweeper or a computer analyst might be different. The interviewer must be flexible.

Candidates are also often judged against one another rather than against set criteria. Thus, a candidate following a very unqualified applicant may appear to be a superstar simply by breathing in cadence; but the interviewer must consider whether or not that individual is really any better qualified for the position.

What most of the above points to is a need to train interviewers how to interview. Few people, if any, are natural interviewers, although they are likely to become more proficient with practice. A line manager who may interview one to three candidates a year cannot be expected to be as skilled as the employment recruiter who interviews all day long. But then, if the recruiter is interviewing incorrectly, it really does not make much difference. It is important, therefore, to consider training all those involved in the interviewing process in good interviewing skills.

Candidates today are sharp. They have been well educated on how to interview, what questions to expect, and how to present themselves. They are schooled and prepared. The interviewer must also be schooled and prepared in order to be effective.

Interviewers must know the requirements of the job. This is where the job description plays a vital role. Interviewers must be in contact with line management to ensure an understanding of exactly what skills a candidate should possess and the relative importance of those skills. They must then structure a set of open-ended questions that cannot be answered yes or no, designed to explore a candidate's experiences and background. This structure, or set of questions, is then used with each candidate for a given position. This approach provides a comparable basis for judging the candidates and focuses on skills necessary for job performance. While this approach cannot totally eliminate personal biases, it can significantly reduce their impact.

Additionally, more than one person should be given the opportunity to interview the candidate, including the employment recruiter, the line manager to whom the candidate will ultimately report, and, if possible, the candidate's peers. The more individuals getting exposure to a candidate, the more effective the hiring decision will be. This effectiveness translates into greater reliability and validity.

While human resource management plays an integral role in locating qualified candidates, its role should be one of advising and recommending. The final hiring decision should be made by the line manager. (Note that the offer should come from personnel to ensure administrative processing is correct.) In spite of the emphasis on skills, in truth it is necessary to ensure a good match between the employer and the employee, which may involve such variables as personalities. The candidate will report to the line manager and that reporting relationship will be enhanced by allowing the line manager to make the final decision. This also makes the line manager responsible for the selection, whether it works or not. If the line manager makes a poor decision, it is not blamed on personnel. This helps to keep relations between personnel and a given department operational.

What a candidate should be told about an organization is another important issue. As the candidate is selling to the recruiter, the recruiter must sell the organization to the candidate. No department in any organization is perfect. Every place has its idiosyncrasies, and these should be explained to the candidate. It is not necessary to share gossip, but a realistic overview is expected. In this overview, candidates should be told about the organization's culture, its environment, the candidate's opportunities for advancement, and how management in the area operates. This is part of treating people humanely and being open in communications. While this sounds easy, it is often not done. Reasons cited for leaving organizations often attest to this oversight.

TRAINING AND DEVELOPMENT

Probably the greatest evolution in human resource management has occurred in the training and development function. What was once the department that trained clerks and first-line supervisors, and coordinated college courses and external seminars for their employees to take, has evolved into a vital component of the organization. This change has also been reflected in its name. The training and development department is now referred to as the human resources development department (HRD). In fact, the importance of HRD has changed so drastically in the 1980s that some propose that shortly the personnel function will report to it, rather than the other way around (Odione1985).

A review of training programs used by organizations shows they vary from simple orientation and those that are legally required, to elaborate configurations that resemble college settings. The hoped-for end result of instituting most training programs is higher output of the final product. In addition to increased output, increased employee motivation and job skills, reduced turnover and grievance rates, and changes in job-related behavior may also result from training (Holoviak 1982).

In whatever form, training has become important as an organizational activity over the past decades. There are various reasons offered for the heightened interest in training activity. First, rapidly changing demands for output and the complexity of modern organizations require increased attention be offered to upgrading human resources. Second, advances in technology have brought with them new work requirements, and employees must acquire sophisticated skills to operate new and complex equipment efficiently. Third, companies are increasingly aware of the importance of providing career-path opportunities for employees. To handle people's career orientation objectives successfully requires that company human relations and/or management training facilities be in place. Fourth, training is a vehicle to counter obsolescence of knowledge and executive burnout, and to help employees who have plateaued or are in dead-end jobs. Finally, training does more than prepare employees for skills required today. It develops areas to address future manpower needs. In doing so, it relates these future needs to the higher standards of employee aspirations and expectations that come with the increased educational levels of today's employees (Henderson 1979, and Beatty and Scheneier 1981).

There has been keen interest in recent years in training by industrial relations researchers and others in related fields. The areas identified as being affected by training have been numerous. For example H. Hand and J. W. Solcum investigated the effects of human relations training on managerial effectiveness (Hand and Solcum 1972), while others have looked at training as a means of confronting blue-collar job behavior and attitude problems (Hautaluoma and Gavin 1975 and Fournier 1978). Raphael suggests that training may be used as a vehicle to control the costly effects of employee turnover (Raphael 1975).

Union and nonunion construction workers were compared along a slightly different research line. The output of the unionized workers was found to be 29 percent greater than that of the nonunion groups. There were two reasons offered to explain this difference. The first dealt with the various hiring functions unions handle that reduce the number of employees and other costs to unionized companies. The other reason was that workers received more training in the unionized setting than their nonunion counterparts (Rosow 1981).

Training offers a strong potential for companies in the U.S. to help reverse the concern about reduced productivity. In a research project conducted by Stephen Holoviak (1982), there appeared to be a relationship between company-sponsored training programs and productivity variations. In fact, it appeared that the greater the percent of management officials exposed to training programs, the higher the company's productivity.

The Holoviak report used coal mine organizations and compared companies using formal (college-type) training, those offering the more traditional managerial training, and companies that supplied no management training to enhance organizational effectiveness. The company-sponsored programs were those conducted by consultants on company premises, and by in-house staff trainers. There were strong differences found with respect to productivity between companies with company-sponsored programs and those that offered no training. Less difference was found between productivity of those using formal programs and those who offer no training. The measure of effectiveness used in the study was output of product for each man day (Holoviak 1982).

In its basic form, human resources development department (HRD) is responsible for the training and development of employees in an organization. In its broadest perspective, it is the catalyst for cultural change in an organization. Human resource development probably touches more people in the organization than any other department and affects them from their first day on the job to the last.

To start, HRD is instrumental in acclimating new employees to the organization. This "new employee orientation" is built around informing new employees of their benefits, company policy, and the expectations of the organization. This program serves many purposes, but its primary focus is to provide a motivational "first impression" of the oganization.

Human resource development is also vitally linked to training efforts. HRD ensures that the training that occurs "addresses the job duties, skills, work performance standards, major procedures, and organizational departmental goals" (Fisher 1985). Meeting this requirement involves many different training programs. These programs encompass secretarial skills, executive development, and all the jobs in-between. They are augmented by various seminars and workshops offered by outside vendors and by university courses. The role of HRD in this context thus becomes one of providing for the immediate and future training and educational needs of the organization.

CAREER PLANNING AND DEVELOPING EMPLOYEES

Human resources development also focuses on the concept of developing employees. Developing employee skills is one aspect of training; however, the development function takes this concept one step further. Development implies growth, and HRD must be the catalyst for employees' personal growth. This activity takes on many forms, but the most obvious is career planning.

Career Planning

Career planning is a process whereby individuals are counseled regarding their career paths. These counseling sessions, coupled with various career development assessment tools, are geared toward providing each employee with a plan regarding a career path and realistic expectation with respect to the organization. Once this plan is made, a series of steps is outlined that will enable the employee to acquire the necessary skills to foster that growth.

Regardless of the position an individual holds in an organization, employees are showing a more aggressive attitude toward the directions of their careers (Gould 1978). In a research study by Holoviak (1984), it was suggested that there is a link between the existence of defined career paths and the effectiveness of the organization.

Data for the Holoviak study were gathered from six underground coal mine organizations. The six coal mine organizations were similar in output of coal, technology utilization, and geographic location. In addition, coal seam characteristics were held constant in order to strengthen comparability between organizations through reducing operating differences due to geological configuration of the coal seam. The six companies broke down into two coal seam groups of three companies each: one soft coal and one metallurgical coal group.

Career paths were identified as a link to company productivity. Career development opportunities, along with a larger group of organizational variables, have been found to differentiate among productivity variations between organizations.

Coal mining companies represent useful laboratories for study for several reasons. First, coal is expected to play an increasingly important role in meeting future energy requirements, yet the industry has been beset with the problem of declining productivity since 1969. Second, the high capital investment required to bring a mine into operation places it in a status comparable to other industries. Third, the history of union management relations in the coal industry presents a classic setting for study of company operations relating to personnel and labor relations policy.

As a means of handling the aggressive attitude of contemporary employees, viable paths can offer a reasonable approach to the realization of employee career expectations. Career paths can insure an adequate supply of trained persons to fill needed jobs. The coal industry experience, involving ineffective manpower forecasting combined with a lack of defined career paths, has resulted in a lack of manager talent and a shortage of skilled production workers (Comptroller General 1977).

In another work, James Walker (1976) cites an additional problem in identifying career paths. He points out that they are traditionally emphasized only for upward mobility within a single occupation or work area. Lateral career paths provide exposure to multiple functions and activities in the company, which can produce workers with broader capabilities for the organization and still be highly satisfying to the employee. A problem that results in frustration to both line and staff work-ers in the coal industry is the absence of movement between the two. Even among the most productive of companies in this study, there is a noticeable absence of lateral transfers, or any transfers, between line and staff functions. Yet, in the research, Walker indicates that an organization with no career path information would see positive results from even the static traditional descriptions.

A link has been established between career paths and many aspects of employee relations, with problems of employee career orientation being a significant factor. Several studies (Hammer and Smith 1978, Eng and Gottsdanker 1979, Miller and Kroll 1970, Thornton 1978, and Constanzaro 1976) discuss a host of various aspects related to career paths. These aspects include levels of unionization activity, self-image, job competency, dead-end jobs, plateaued career positions, turnover, work effect, and status levels.

Data gathered from the six coal mine organizations along the two coal seam descriptions suggest that the use of career path orientation may provide a vehicle to tie its presence to increased organization effectiveness (Table 3-1).

For companies A_1, A_2 and B_2, career paths are defined in a clear and discernible manner (Table 3-1). Among those with lower productivity ratings, there was little evidence of using any sort of career orientation for managers or production workers. Managers from the lower-ranked organizations indicated the lack of defined paths afforded little opportunity for them to grow professionally and become more responsible as managers.

As mentioned earlier, there were other points examined in organization structure that are also believed to have interrelated effects. There were not sufficient data to attribute an exact degree of productivity variance associated with only the area of career path utilization. Yet, efforts extended into providing career path opportunities for workers has tended to show up as a link to organization effectiveness in various ways.

One of the more current issues surrounding and complicating current career development planning is the realization that it is built on a growth premise. Positions at the upper levels in organizations are becoming more scarce. As organizations trimmed off excess baggage, one of the greatest cuts was

TABLE 3.1.
Presence of Defined Career Paths Compared to Productivity

Observation	Productivity[a]	Defined Career Paths[b]
Seam group I[c]		
A_1	12.72	Yes
B_1	6.98	No
C_1	6.40	No
Seam group II[c]		
A_2	9.28	d
B_2	7.42	Yes
C_2	6.12	No

[a]Productivity is output/man-day in terms of tons of coal.
[b]Based on thirty-three observations.
[c]Seam Group I — Coal used in electrical generation. Seam Group II—metallurgical used coal.
[d]Company A_2 is in process of transition to different organization structure, included in the structure change is to define career paths.
Source: *Performance and Instruction Journal 23*, no. 7 (1984): 8. Reprinted with permission.

in the middle- to upper-management ranks. With fewer positions being available at the top and fewer vacancies expected in the future, employees must be counseled realistically with respect to the probability that they will reach those positions. In addition, the work force is seeking trade-offs with respect to leisure and work. Most of human relations activities have traditionally assumed that everyone wants to "get to the top." Getting to a management position , or "to the top," requires many sacrifices. Many workers are not willing to make these sacrifices, e.g., working a fourteen-hour day, constant geographic relocation, or even the stress associated with the job itself. With this in mind, career development should be considered from a broader perspective, assisting people in their specific career objectives so they remain motivated during their worklife. These two issues, fewer management positions and more leisure desired, indicate some of the reasons career counseling is becoming so specialized in organizations.

To counter both of the issues mentioned above, career counseling must become more sophisticated. The sophistication lies in a realistic approach plus a coordinated tie to the organization as a whole. This means that career counseling must not be done in a vacuum. Systems must be in place in the organization to ensure internal mobility. This activity has to be linked to the human resource planning system, which we said earlier must closely align itself with organizational strategic plans.

Equally important is the guidance the employee receives. Each employee is entitled to accurate feedback about performance and realistic expectations with respect to career growth within the organization. Time must be spent with each employee to ascertain attitudes toward a number of things, for instance a desire for responsibility in the organization. Coupled with this discussion, too, must be an open and honest explanation of the possibility of the employee reaching various positions in the organization. This means each employee's skill level must be accurately assessed and put into its proper perspective. Those with high potential need to be identified and set on an appropriate course of action. Those without high potential also need a course of action. The difference will be in how the organization views employees, its philosophical beliefs with regard to career development, and its willingness to assist workers in reaching their own levels of maximization. These could be represented as promotions into positions of higher responsibility, lateral transfers, job enhancement, compensation systems to support increased salaries without moving up the "corporate ladder," or adequately preparing workers to move out of the organization into other organizations where there may be a better fit.

ORGANIZATION AND DEVELOPMENT

The last major component, but certainly not the least, of HRD is organization development (OD). OD is defined as "a long-range effort to improve problem solving and the effectiveness of intact work teams" (Fiedler and Garcia 1985). Achieving this goal requires many interventions designed to address environment issues in the organization. Environment issues, or culture, include such things as how individuals are valued in the organization (assets or machines), how people relate to one another in the organization (competitively or collaboratively), how decisions are made (autocratically or participatively), and how communication takes place (rigid and formal or flexible and informal). While any intervention is designed to improve the existing culture, it is not done to imply right or wrong, only to develop what is appropriate in effective and efficient organizations. However, with the impact that

Tom Peters and Bob Waterman have had with *In Search of Excellence*, the reality is that the more "excellent" organizations are those that support the employees. The top management of such organizations support the treatment of workers as assets, not things.

Achieving these goals is not easy. Change in any organization is difficult and the difficulty is compounded when trying to change the ways of a long-standing regime. Regardless of the difficulty, the need for change has never been so apparent as it has been in the 1980s. Competition, lower productivity, and other factors have all called attention to the concept that the members of the organization must be focused on one goal— the organization's betterment—not focusing on individual aspirations. This premise attacks, however, the use of politics that occurs in companies. And that is a major challenge.

Probably the best-known intervention is the teambuilding process. A series of experiential learnings assists in facilitating this process. The process is based on the premise that all individuals are different and that each brings a unique set of skills into a job. It is because of these differences that problems may occur. These differences can also provide the cornerstones of success. Teambuilding focuses on building positively on individual differences. No one can expect everyone in an organization to like one another. That is not the goal of teambuilding. Its goal, rather, is to leave personality differences behind, focus on the task, and work together to achieve a mutually accepted goal. This takes time, patience, and a strong leader at the executive level who is not going to accept anything less.

EMPLOYEE RELATIONS

Employee relations activities in an organization are varied. Some are oriented toward ensuring that open communications take place while others are aimed at developing and implementing corporate policies. Employee relations is also very active in ensuring that complaint procedures exist for employees in unionized organizations, called the grievance procedure. It is important to make a distinction between labor relations and employee relations. Often, companies have one or the other, but not both. On the surface, both conduct many of the same activities, i.e., counseling employees on performance problems, facilitating the grievance procedure, and maintaining corporate policies. The biggest difference lies in the area of flexibility. Employee relations departments face fewer constraints than labor relations departments, which must deal with representing a union. The degree of these constraints is contingent on the terms and conditions of the agreed-upon contract. It has been said that employee relations is what you do when no union is present—fail at employee relations and you will have labor relations.

ORGANIZATION COMMUNICATIONS

Organization communications is a catch-all phrase used to describe many activities in the organization. It encompasses how workers are being treated by management; how information is being disseminated to employees; and how workers perceive the culture, working conditions, and complaint/grievance procedures. This multi-faceted approach rests on the idea that people can talk to one another. Differences may arise, but a mechanism should be in place to mediate them before they become major disasters.

This process involves having various programs operating that give workers exposure to and information from top management on the "state of affairs." It is built around the belief that employees are an important asset and that without them the organization would cease to exist. Imagine all General Motors employees quitting in one day. Obviously, this would place GM in serious difficulty.

Organization communications is also built on the belief that workers should have some say in respect to the quality of work life. Employees are probably the best source of information regarding happenings and operations in an organization. Accordingly, they need to be polled periodically, randomly perhaps, to obtain a perspective on how the work force is doing. This quick assessment also gives workers the opportunity to vent any problems they are experiencing. This venting provides an avenue for investigating problems in their early stages so they can be rectified with a minimal amount of disruption.

Organization communications also advocates a means for employees to make suggestions to make operations more effective. The idea behind company suggestion programs, quality circles, et cetera, is to give the worker the opportunity to make recommendations to correct inefficiencies. In addition, this process provides an opportunity to recognize employees' contributions. This results in employees' becoming more aware of their surroundings. Some companies provide incentives, such as monetary awards. These are usually based on some percentage of the first year's savings. While there are too many facets of corporate communications to identify all of them here, those that have been considered provide a good basis for developing effective communications.

Rumors in organizations, be they true or unfounded, serve no purpose. They result in office gossip, downtime, and a loss of productivity. If for no other reason, companies should have a sound corporate communications program so workers do not have to search for information. That time spent searching is costing the organization money. At its best, good corporate communication fosters sound management and a culture supportive of its workers.

OTHER EMPLOYEE RELATIONS ACTIVITIES

Certainly the importance of communications cannot be overstated. It permeates all parts of the organization. But employee relations departments do much more than ensure that corporate communications are sound. First of all, they are generally responsible for researching, writing, and implementing sound personnel policies. Appropriate procedures and rules need to be put together in reference manuals and given to all employees. In addition, personnel policies must be reviewed annually, and updated by making necessary additions or deletions. Employee relations must also ensure that the information is written in such a manner that it is understood. Writing in jargon or legalese serves no purpose, since personnel policy manuals are written for the employees' benefit.

Employee relations is also responsible for some of the more traditional functions of the past, namely employee activities. These activities, to name a few, include company-sponsored sporting events; various clubs, such as tennis and golf; annual service awards banquets; and the United Way Campaign. Most of these tend to be leisure activities, but reflect a genuine interest in the well-rounded well-being of the employee.

More recently, employee relations departments have focused on stress management issues and employee assistance programs.

WHERE IS TRADITIONAL HUMAN RESOURCE MANAGEMENT GOING?

At the onset of this chapter, it was indicated that human resources has undergone significant changes over the last two decades. What can be expected in the future is that more change will occur. Human resource management is quickly becoming more prominent in organizations. Until recently, it was almost unheard of for a human resource management person to be part of top management. But with the new emphasis in organizations on valuing the workers as assets, more and more organizations are placing human resource executives in top management where they can be involved in decisions about the general welfare of workers.

Cultural change will no doubt continue into the 1990s. Organizations are restructuring and refocusing to ensure a customer service orientation. Turning this perception around is one of the major tasks of the organization, a task well facilitated with the assistance of human resource management.

Furthermore, one can expect to see new ways of doing business. Organizations are going to need to find alternative work methods. Job redesign, work enhancements, and cottage industries—or work at home concepts— are sure to occur. Automation is quickly entering all aspects of organizations. There will be a need to find ways to help displaced workers. More and more companies are looking at ways of "outplacing" employees whose jobs have been eliminated through no fault of their own. Companies are looking for ways to handle this issue, both from a moral point of view and from the point of view that handling it effectively will benefit the organization.

Lastly, there will be continuing efforts on the part of human resource management to contain benefit costs. Skyrocketing costs cannot be borne by the organization. The biggest item, health care benefits, must be reviewed, with an eye to lower-cost insurers, alternative offerings, and increasing each employee's paid share. With the advent of computer-assisted human resource systems, companies need to explore more cafeteria benefit offerings. In this manner, employees can choose the benefits they want and simultaneously reduce benefit costs.

Human resource management itself must be automated. Human resource departments have computer-assisted systems available called **Human Resource Information Systems (HRIS)**.

These enable them to capture more information about employees, store it, and have it available for efficient retrieval. Many of the routine administrative processes can be automated, and in so doing increase the productivity of human resource management itself.

SUMMARY

As we enter the mid-1990s, what once was "personnel" may no longer be recognized. Its role in the organization, its function, and its operations will have drastically changed. However, one important piece will remain, and that is the focus of human resources. Its primary concern will still be people, and how to make their jobs more meaningful, more productive, and more rewarding.

The importance of compensation and benefit administration in an organization cannot be overstated. Much of the thrust of the organization rests on its work. We have seen how the job analysis process affects all aspects of human resources and the organization as a whole, and how usage structures and benefit administration are ever-changing.

This chapter has included a look at personnel planning, the search for candidates, and the interviewing process. Training and development have also been discussed. We have explored human resource development—past, present, and future. Human resource development has changed its focus drastically over the past decade, and is expected to be the forerunner in implementing changes to come. This work, however, does not yet exist.

One of the major elements of successful intervention is communications. A process of ensuring that organizational communications is efficient and effective is also explored. Employee relations serves as the most general component of human resources. It includes many activities, but the most notable of these is the corporate communications process. The effectiveness of this process alone can be a determining factor as to whether employees unite together and seek third party representation, or work well with management one-on-one.

Four specific functions in human resources management have been isolated. Human resources is explained in this quadrant mode because it appears to be representative of how the major functions in human resources are divided. But this is not to say that in every case the demarcation is this clear. In some instances, one individual may be responsible for the entire gamut, whereas in others, different combinations may exist. For instance, it is not that uncommon to see employment and training in one department, as well as variations like compensation and training together. Whatever way they are grouped, however, the activities that must be performed remain the same.

II   The New Wave: Current Challenges

Part II looks at some of the current corporate activities that are producing solid results—results that make the people feel a part of the organization and contribute to increased organization effectiveness. This is not a discussion about passing fads, but rather proven concepts that should endure well into the future.

This part begins with Chapter 4, which discusses worker participation in running the organization. And, it offers some of the latest research findings regarding such areas as quality circles, which, when managed correctly, can be productive and effective in helping manage the human resource investment. Chapter 5 tells how to manage organization stress effectively and identify its signs not just in managers, but at all levels in the organization. The last chapter in this part, Chapter 6, deals with the exciting potential offered by employee counseling. This tool may be an effective means for handling some common problems like absenteeism, tardiness, and similar problems in a positive fashion.

4   Quality Circles: Can We Work Together?

INTRODUCTION

Traditionally, business relations between management and labor in the United States have been adversarial, with both sides exercising their influence through union organization or legal powers. And for more than 50 years, the American Labor Movement pursued objectives within U.S. industry that did require an adversarial approach. Labor was fighting for safe and humane working conditions, health benefits to protect its membership, retirement security, and equitable wages so that its laborers could share the profits being realized by industrial management.

OBJECTIVES OF QUALITY CIRCLES

Many business people contemplating the use of quality circles expect to experience a savings in a near-term perspective (e.g., the next fiscal quarter). However, the objectives of quality circle programs cannot be expressed in terms of short-run dollars saved (although that is frequently a pleasant side effect). The objectives of quality circles are

1) to enhance the quality of management in the organization;
2) to gain access to the problem-solving skills of the employees; and
3) to enhance job satisfaction and quality of work life (Schuster 1985.)

ORIGINS OF THOUGHT ON QUALITY CIRCLES

Following World War II, U.S. business and manufacturing dominated the world marketplace as the most productive nation in the world. Not only were the goods produced consumed within our own country, but also nations abroad were supplied with many of their consumable and durable products. Since the U.S. was virtually the only major supplier, the quality of goods was not as important a factor as other criteria, including design, technology, functionality, and price. Since what was produced sold easily, there was no impetus to improve the quality of products. Statistics for this decade reveal that the productivity rate in the country was growing by three percent per year, a rate that generally gives evidence of an overall increase in the standard of living, a strong market, and a favorable climate for business. The implicit message throughout U.S. industry was that, without competition, it could be profitable to produce less than top quality goods.

While the United States enjoyed this profitable position in the marketplace, Japan on the other hand suffered a reputation of being the mass producer of junk merchandise. Following the Second World War, Japan realized that it could not rebuild its country and economy by manufacturing poor quality products. It was still being occupied by the Allies and much of the country's operations were monitored and controlled by the government established by General Douglas MacArthur. Senior managers and plant directors were removed from their positions after the war as a way of checking the post-war growth that would occur. Many of the new young managers who were put in charge of manufacturing facilities did not have the experience and knowledge to lead the business world in their struggling first attempts at reconstruction. As a beginning step, a Japanese coalition was formed in 1950 called JUSE, the Japanese Union of Scientists and Engineers, whose main function was to promote quality control activities in industry. It has become the parent organization for the country's more than 10 million quality circles.

According to Bank and Wilpert (1983), quality circle development then took on a formal and planned schedule of growth within Japanese manufacturing. U.S. involvement sparked much of the activity, as we were consultants to their businesses, and colleagues to the score of young managers educated at institutions in the United States. The use of quality circles to aid the development of the manufacturing system in Japan can be described in five stages:

1) Between 1945 and 1950 U.S. advisors and Japanese managers begin investigations and research to apply control techniques to Japanese industry; the Allied Forces organize a quality control study group.

2) Between 1950 and 1955 statistical methods were used in quality control activities; W. Edwards Deming, a U.S. consultant, began to teach statistical quality control technique courses. JUSE and the Japan Standard Association (JSA) begin training seminars and work-related courses on quality control and operations research. The Japan Productivity Center was established by the cooperative efforts of government and private corporations. Deming advocated that quality control specialists in a separate department could function in a general capacity throughout the plant operations.

3) The high-growth years between 1955 and 1963 evidenced a net increase in productivity that surpassed 10 percent annually. Industrial output tripled as a new campaign toward increased quality and productivity was set in place, involving line managers in the efforts. Joseph Juran, another American consultant, also argued that quality control had to be considered in the context of general management staff.

4) Quality circles emerged for the first time during the period from 1960 to 1965. They swept through many areas of operations and involved supervisors, foremen, workers, and all levels of management. Kaoru Ishikawa emerged as the Japanese proponent for "quality" leadership. He emphasized group decentralization, participative decision-making, group problem-solving and extensive employee training to emphasize the new approach to job involvement.

5) Throughout the period from 1965 to 1970, quality circle concepts techniques spread extensively through every level of the manufacturing organization. National quality circle activities were organized and efforts to promote the quality circle concept in the United States were made by Japanese managers visiting our manufacturing sites.

MEASUREMENT OF RESULTS

Measurement of the results of a quality circle program creates difficulties for U.S organizations. For whatever reason, be it academic training or cultural background, there is a compulsion among U.S. managers to compare results to some percentage return on investment. If this cannot be done, upper-level managers feel insecure about supporting programs that do not lend themselves to accurate measurement.

It is difficult to measure the interaction of human variables in the workplace as accurately as the production rates of machines, the effects of new technology, the interaction of a new parts retrieval system, or other such factors. It is difficult to hold such factors as attitudes, peer relationships, employee service programs, incentive programs, career programs, and the like constant for study while adjusting other environmental factors.

In a study by Paula Kirby and Stephen Holoviak (1985) to investigate the content and extent of program evaluations for quality circles, several revealing facts came to light. First, there is no obvious trend in the collection or measurement of the effects of quality circle programs in the workplace. There is some guidance available in the literature on this topic, yet practitioners do not follow these recommendations. Second, 28 percent of the survey respondents collected no information on the quality circle programs. Even among those that collected information, no trend was present as to distribution of the data. Such a lack of evaluation of the activity of the program in the work environment is a serious problem. Organizations monitor other investment programs. Certainly the investment in human activity for organization improvement merits a similar output of energy. Third, 22 percent of the research group has no measures of the effects of job quality on productivity whatsoever. And only 21.6 percent of the respondents attempted to measure any changes in productivity as a result of activity of a quality circle program.

Results of quality circle programs can be measured in any number of ways. For example: 1) increased productivity, 2) identified cost reductions, 3) improved communications, 4) decreased absenteeism, 5) decreased tardiness, 6) decreased waste, scraps, etc., and 7) increased performance appraisals, teamwork, and job knowledge. Achievement of any number of these will result in cost savings over time.

For the concept of quality circles to work in any organization, there has to be a dedication to quality from the top down. However, for long-term success the literature suggests the program be based on voluntary bottom-up action by rank-and-file employees. The indications from early research suggest that management support be highly visible, but without forced employee participation.

Quality circles result in many benefits for both managers and circle members. Successful business arrangements indicate that both parties must feel they have benefited from participation. For managers such benefits include: 1) better employee morale, 2) improved safety records, 3) better teamwork, 4) enhanced product quality, and 5) better employee relations. In similar fashion, benefits to circle members include: 1) better communications with supervisors, 2) better problem awareness, 3) better awareness of the status quo of the organization, 4) improved working environment, and 5) circle members have a better chance of learning new skills (List 1982).

The topic of benefits frequently leads to discussion of rewards for circle members. There is not systematic research conducted on this topic as it relates to the U.S. experience. Yet, there is guidance with respect to compensation theory; and the experience of Japan, Germany, and other nations.

Research indicates that financial rewards are of limited use for productivity plans and worker participation plans. Most compensation experts agree that concentrating on money is antithetical to the concept of becoming part of the organization. Sound compensation theory suggests that long-term savings will result in real wage increases to employees. The most successful rewards for circle participants are recognition by management and peers of the individual's contributions—that is, positive reinforcement in terms of praise and recognition.

THE GROUPS INVOLVED

Each party to a quality circle approaches the circle program with different expectations. Likewise there are expectations with respect to the contributions of others. The typical unionized setting has certain roles in mind for managed unions and circle participants.

THE ROLE OF MANAGERS AND SUPERVISORS

Managers and supervisors are expected to be supportive of the program and are urged not to expect quick results. In addition, as circle members, they are expected to be willing to join in and help the program.

Managers should be aware that it takes two for trust to build between the parties and for employees to be convinced that this is a sincere change in managerial approach. Supervisors may serve as a vehicle to bring in people from other departments (employee relations, staff development, et cetera). From time to time it will be necessary for the supervisors to assist in training circle members to handle a task they wish to pursue.

A problem faced in the U.S. that is not found to be a problem in Japan is the impact of quality circles on middle-level managers. Managers are urged to accept the idea that workers are valuable in the development of ideas, and that

1) circle programs will not diminish their power or authority;
2) supervisors can benefit from solutions to long-term problems; and
3) successful quality circles can enhance their career possibilities (Schuster 1985).

There is no need for supervisors to feel threatened about results from a team of workers.

THE ROLE OF UNIONS

In the early stages of the circle movement, unions felt threatened by such activity, which is an understandable response based on a history of adversarial relationships. It is also understandable when the list of managerial fads is considered. Quality circles could easily be perceived as falling into this realm.

However, the current trend of union participation is quite different. For many unions, participation has enhanced their image with members and raised their position versus lowering it as originally feared.

The benefits of cooperation more than outweighed those of hostility. Everyone perceives that the survival of both parties, union and company, may be at stake. In addition, several unions now view cooperation as a technique to attract the white collar, well-educated worker.

THE ROLE OF EMPLOYEES

The participation and activity of employees has been viewed from several vantage points already. One important point has to do with who guides the circle. Due to the voluntary nature of the program, insisting on supervisors to be heads of circles may jeopardize the long-term health of the program. For some, the supervisor is the natural person to head the circle since he/she is the person responsible in that particular area.

Managers must ensure to the satisfaction of members that their ideas will not result in layoffs. For many organizations it can be just the opposite. Ideas can result in jobs saved.

ESTABLISHING A QUALITY CIRCLE PROGRAM

The menu of steps to establish a quality circle varies with several factors:

1) Degree of sophistication of managers.
2) Amount of formal management training.
3) Type of organization, current managerial structure.

Certainly each consultant involved will offer a different number of steps. Yet all must cover the same topic, the depth of coverage depending on the above three items. The first item refers to the degree to which the staff is skilled in handling the collection and utilization of data. The second factor is concerned with the amount of formal managerial training the staff has been or is currently exposed to, which may result in unnecessary duplication of training effort on when and how much training was received. Finally, the organization structure can reveal a great deal of information. If the structure is autocratic, then the transition to a participative style will be difficult for some and take a longer and more intensive effort.

STEPS IN THE PROCESS OF ESTABLISHING A PROGRAM

The process of implementing a program offered here is a generic menu based on the assumption that significant levels of training for both staff and participants is necessary for success of the program.

Step One: Meeting With Union Representatives. Depending on the degree of cooperation between the parties, this step can be very helpful or just pro forma. However, the step is still necessary in the interest of harmonious future cooperation.

Step Two: Staff Training. If a quality circle program becomes an effective extension of management efforts, then new patterns of dialogue will emerge between employees and staff managers. It is important to train and prepare them in this development effort. The typical contents of staff training include

1) description and purpose of quality circles;
2) new methodology to handle discipline, complaints, and employee questions;
3) conflict resolution and stress management;
4) communications skills;
5) management counseling techniques; and
6) basic information on employee relations.

Step Three: Establishment of a Steering Committee. The steering committee for a quality circle makes policy decisions; develops the philosophy and objectives under which it operates, and provides guidance, support, needed resources, and a visible display of management support.

A steering committee is comprised of people who represent various functional areas and who are usually mid- and upper-level managers. It may also include the chief operating officers. The steering committee hears the circle reports and formal presentations; works closely with the facilitator for the program; and, during initial start-up of a program, meets weekly. Once a program is established, the committee can meet bi-monthly. It is helpful to have a rotation schedule of the committee, that is, staggered terms of participation, so more management staff can participate and yet continuity can be preserved.

For participants, a steering committee is part of the guarantee that someone is listening. Everyone has given suggestions to supervisors. Whether or not these suggestions get further attention may be quite arbitrary. This is not the case with a steering committee.

Step Four: Training and Selecting Facilitators and Circle Leaders. The facilitator can be the key to the success of the program. When there are several circles operating, facilitator becomes the equivalent of a half-time position. Duties of a facilitator include: forming necessary links between circle programs and the internal organizations; locating specialists to assist the circle group with special problems; keeping accurate records; coordinating circle activities; working with, and being a member of, the steering committee; helping members with problems; and attending all circle meetings.

A facilitator should be trained and have the necessary skills in cognitive, problem-solving techniques normally used in quality circles; problem identification; data locations and gathering; problem analysis; and the ability to present findings. Furthermore, a facilitator should possess consultative skills, communication skills, and teambuilding and conflict management skills. The facilitator can acquire the balance of necessary skills through involvement in the staff and participant training.

Circle leaders can be selected by the steering committee or the circle group itself. The best approach is for the facilitator to ask for volunteers because a successful leader will be someone that wants the position. The leader should be enthusiastic about the program and be able to work well with people in order to gain measurable results. Normal participant training, if complete, should be sufficient. The circle leader can be the supervisor. Although some companies insist the circle leader be a manager, many experts do not believe that it is necessary.

Step Five: Training for Participants. Involvement in a quality circle will necessitate the utilization of many skills. Unfortunately, not all participants come to the program with equal skills and experience. Therefore, it becomes important to provide the necessary training for the volunteers to ensure this equity. Furthermore, the pre-circle involvement training serves as a vehicle to enhance employee skills to the total benefit of the company. In many cases, this pre-training alone will increase the efficiency of the organization. The training scenario for participants includes

1) description and purpose of a quality circle, including the scope of issues to discuss and expectations of what can be accomplished;
2) training in the organization of the company, so that participants' suggestions will be based on a clearer understanding of the structure and its operations;
3) training and communication skills;
4) human resource training, including some basics in employee relations;
5) explanation of group dynamics;
6) explanation of conflict resolution;
7) training in information and data gathering and utilization; and,
8) training in how to make presentations (Dewer 1980 and Nellis 1985).

The initial quality circle meeting is used to identify and define topics of concentration. The group's regular schedule should consist of an hour-long meeting once a week before or after work and should be paid time. Alternatively, the meetings can be held during regular working hours. However, because jobs often involve necessary task completion, pulling a worker off the job may be difficult.

THE REASONS FOR PROGRAM DIFFICULTY

As would be suspected, deciding to have a quality circle program and going through the "steps" to implement it correctly do not guarantee success. Listed below are possible causes, offered by writers in the field, of some failures:

1) *Impatience.* With the high cost of implementation, management often expects too rapid a return on investment. If there has been a history of an adversarial type of relationship between labor and management, trust between the parties may take a reasonable period of time to materialize.
2) *Lack of management support.* For a program to be successful, it must be supported by top management and middle management, including responsiveness to circle suggestions.

3) *Absence of objectives for the program.*
4) *Lack of program publicity to the workers.* People must be informed. This will contribute to confidence in the program and information-gathering efforts.
5) *No recognition.* People like to be recognized for their achievements.

SUMMARY OF CURRENT PERSPECTIVES

During the 1970s several companies in the United States were beginning quality circle programs based on the impressive results of nearly one million circles operating in Japan. According to Mohr (1983), the Japanese circles are reputed to solve three to four problems per year per circle. At an average cost savings to their company of $5,000 per problem (conservatively $15,000 per year per circle), Japan as a nation is saving upwards of $5 billion per year as a result of quality circle activity. Since many of these savings are cumulative, that is, saved year after year, their effect on the company exercises a very strong impact. When estimates were made in 1978, after quality circles had been in existence for sixteen years, it was estimated that the total cumulative savings were $50 billion.

Lockheed Missiles and Space Company, Honeywell, Inc., and Hughes Aircraft set up the first U.S. quality circles, which served as models for employee involvement programs that soon followed at other major U.S. companies. Westinghouse, Harley-Davidson, Sperry Corporation, RCA, IBM, General Motors, and Babcock and Wilcox all began their programs around 1974. Other organizations such as the U.S. Air Force, Army, and Navy public agencies soon developed similar quality circle activities. The presence of quality circle-type activities in many enterprises, private and public, attests to their success and to the support offered by workers, both managers and employees.

Naisbitt and Aburdeen's book, *Reinventing the Corporation,* (1984) suggests that the message of quality circles has registered in a larger way, very unlike the impact it had during the period from the 1920s to the 1960s. Instead of being an obscure management technique confined to the world of operations or manufacturing administration, the idea behind the technique has pervaded much of the spirit of our 1980s culture. Naisbitt and Aburdeen offer ten considerations that will help individuals transform themselves (and their company) for the new information society. Each of the ten guidelines contains a truth essential to the successful operation of a quality circle program. Each guideline also suggests the spirit or value set necessary in a workplace for participative management to occur. The emphasis of the entire text is placed to highlight the individual's contribution to the workplace.

No matter how businesses are altered, whether through technologies, product lines, financial structures, or marketing plans, the way of managing human resources remains a crucial factor that pervades all other factors. Analysis of data as far back as 1929 consistently shows human factors are the major source of growth in individual earnings, institutional productivity, and national income (Carnevale 1986). Moreover, the same data demonstrate clearly that "working smarter"—a general theme for quality circle teams—is the most significant among human factors in producing income and productivity growth. Projections of economic growth through the 1980s, based on U.S. Department of Commerce Data, show similar patterns.

The Conference Board (1984) conducted a study to determine the qualitative ways in which companies undertake innovations in human resource management. Surveys, interviews, and questionnaires yielded data showing that most of the executives and practitioners consulted believe that the experience now being gained in participative management and quality of work life efforts will yield a reliable alternative managerial style, necessary for the future of United States productivity. Other data from the study provide some clear directions for where we must head to help quality circle-type activities grow into a more secure, participative system.

1) *Program Viability.* Because the participative style is often too little understood, training must occur to familiarize all plant personnel with its implications. The organizational changes should not be structured so as to appear to be another short-run gimmick. The designs for group participation should be long-term in nature so as to continue to generate new ideas in a wide variety of functional areas.

2) *Group Problem Solving.* The problem solving process must be integrated into the way business is managed. In order to circumvent short-term gains, to pursue longer-term and more significant changes, the problem-solving process should be able to influence the organization as a whole.

3) *Management Issues.* Since middle management is the greatest obstacle in securing acceptance and commitment to the new participative work plan, several strategies are recommended. Earlier and

more intensive preparation of middle- and lower-level managers for changes in the organizational culture is required. Companies must also direct their efforts to identify managers and supervisors with high potential for managing participativeness.

4) *White Collar Participation.* It is said that participative work systems are more difficult for the white collar professional to adjust to; the team concept is unfamiliar to them and they perceive themselves as individual problem solvers. But since they compose the majority of the work force (by the year 2000, they will compose 80 percent of the work force), it is important to involve them in employee participation programs. Their potential for increasing overall productivity is enormous.

5　Stress: Under the Gun

INTRODUCTION

Performance problems of once productive, long-term employees and the anguish experienced because efforts to help these employees seem useless are among the most difficult activities in management—activities that are made necessary by stress.

In this chapter, stress, how it impacts the organization, and its most drastic form—burnout—are addressed. One of the newer practices to enter organizations the past few years—Employee Assistance Programs—will also be explored. The realization that stress is prevalent in all organizations has been generally acknowledged. But a further look into this topic is needed. The cause for these problems is not new. Stress is something we all know about. How stress is impacting the organization and how to manage stress are new and important concerns in management today.

Throughout this chapter, the word stress is used to mean something that negatively impacts an individual. It is also important to recognize that stress does have some positive attributes. First of all, stress is energy. Without it, a person can become lethargic, lazy, and inactive. Accordingly, some stress is absolutely necessary. It is stress that causes one to take action and meet challenges. Stress provides the inner energy to reach peak performance when needed. For example, consider a professional athlete before a big game. They "get psyched." This "psyching" is nothing more than high energy vis-a-vis stress. Stress becomes problematic when the energy leads to distress. It is this distress or "stress" that is the focus of this chapter.

Stress must be managed. Considering stress on a bell curve diagram (Figure 5.1), our efforts need to focus on reducing stress on either end of the continuum so that most stress will fall in the middle area—managed stress.

WHAT IS STRESS?

Stress comes in many different forms. In its broadest terms, according to LaGreca (1985), "stress is the mental and physical condition that results from a perceived threat of danger and a pressure to remove it." An interesting point to note about stress is that it comes from some perception about an event that may occur. While this anxiety can be the same for something that may be regarded as being a pleasant event (e.g., getting married) or for a negative experience (e.g., getting fired), the outcome is the same. This outcome results in increased physical problems, such as headaches, ulcers, heart attacks, and generally increased problems at work, such as lower performance evaluation. Knowing that this can result, why do people let it happen? Most people know how it feels when things seem unmanageable. Where do those feelings get their beginnings? Consider some of the more likely candidates for causes of stress.

Probably the biggest concern most people have is the fear that they will fail in an activity. What that activity is varies. It is as much a source of worry to fear losing one's ability to do a job, or not being successful on a new assignment, as it is to failure in a marriage. In all these instances, people are under

FIGURE 5.1. Stress Levels

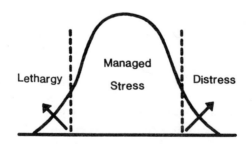

stress, which if not managed may actually result in pressure and negative thinking that can actually bring on the failure they fear.

Fear and negative thinking only make the situation intensify. Allowing this kind of pressure to build can inhibit the ability to see things clearly and handle the situation effectively. Most people dread that phone call from the boss when he says, "Can you come to my office immediately?" They expect the worst to happen, especially if this has happened before and the experience was negative the first time. The moment they hang up they can feel their blood pressure changing. LaGreca (1985) suggests that a physical change does occur: "Your heart rate and blood pressure increase, sugar enters the bloodstream, blood is pumped to the muscles of limbs, and they become tense in readiness for action." These changes are stress.

While stress can be functional, in that it can help one to handle "dangerous" situations, it is often nonfunctional, or actually dysfunctional. Often people allow themselves to feel stress in situations where it is not necessary. Consider for example the case of a graduate student, who experienced panic when a major research paper was returned with no grade, just the words, "See me," written by the instructor. This student became red in the face and began to sweat profusely. On the class break the student approached the instructor and said, "This was my paper, I didn't cheat!" Interestingly enough, this student had been singled out because of the excellent nature of the report. During the meeting with the instructor, the student was told about the exemplary paper and that the note was there because the instructor intended to talk about having the student publish the work.

The above suggests that it is often the uncertainty of a situation that causes the greatest stress. One way that an individual could deal with situations involving uncertainty would be to imagine the worst possible scenario. Assume an individual has made a major mistake at work and is called into the boss's office. Will the boss be upset? Probably. Could the individual be fired? Maybe. If fired, could the individual find work elsewhere in a period of time? Probably. Can the individual die over this? Doubtful. So why worry? The worst thing that could happen is being fired. That is something people recover from. Going through this "down-side" scenario can help to secure uncertainty and the attendant negative thinking and stress. This is easier said than done, but mental imaging can reduce a lot of stress, which, if not managed, affects lives negatively.

As indicated above, there are as many causes of stress as there are activities in life. Fear of failure was identified as a major cause, but there are others that are just as problematic. These others could be categorized as those at work and those at home.

The "at work" causes would take an entire encyclopedia just to list. The world of work is so full of imperfections that almost anything can cause someone problems and stress. Considering work-related stress globally, however, some key problem areas emerge.

One of these problem areas is poor management. Management that is autocratic in decision making, totally task-oriented, and is concerned only with short-run "bottom line" results can cause others stress. Working for a boss who exhibits the above characteristics or in a situation where there are significant personality differences can also lead to stress. Feelings that a job provides no challenge or no room for growth can also lead to high anxiety on the job. Poor communications on the job may also be stressful, making individuals feel left out of the mainstream of activities. And finally, especially in organizations that are changing, new tasks, new reporting relationships, new rules, new regulations, and new procedures can cause a lot of stress. People being displaced due to technological or organizational changes may have particularly difficult stress-related problems.

Organizations must be willing to help alleviate situations that create stress and to establish programs that help employees manage stress. It is important that humanistic processes be in place, including outplacement help, generous severance pay, and medical benefits continuation for a period of time.

While the above list is not exhaustive, it does reflect the stressors that can occur at work. Later in this chapter some stress reduction techniques and the Employee Assistance Program are examined.

The "at home" excuses, too, are many and varied to consider in any detail. It should suffice at this point to suggest that stress at home is eventually going to surface on the job. Managing this category of stress will be addressed in the section on the Employee Assistance Program.

BURNOUT, THE NEW ORGANIZATIONAL KILLER

Burnout is quickly becoming the buzzword of the 1980s. It is a condition brought about by many factors, the primary one of which is stress. The occurrence of stress does not necessarily mean that burnout is also occurring. Burnout has been described by Bruce Baldwin (1985) as a "syndrome resulting from an emotionally destructive relationship to work in which a progressive loss of control, the deterioration of non-work interests, and mixed symptoms reflecting stress overload and depression result in decreased productivity and general life dissatisfaction." This syndrome is brought about by placing all emphasis on one's work, one's career, or one's career aspirations, resulting in inadequate time to "rejuvenate emotionally" (Baldwin 1985). An example would be an individual who works six days a week, twelve hours a day, and never takes a vacation to relax or be with family. This individual is on a burnout course. The adage that "all work and no play makes Johnny dull" has now been revised to read "all work and no play burns Johnny out."

An inherent desire for materialistic goods, status, and organizational power have placed people on a crash course in an attempt to succeed—often at the price of physical health.

How people manage themselves, their time, and their careers may throw them into the throes of burnout. They often do not recognize it until it is too late. Some of the major characteristics of a potential burnout victim are:

1) Burnout candidates experience predominately stress caused by job-related stress.
2) Burnout candidates tend to be idealistic and/or self-motivated achievers.
3) Burnout candidates tend to seek unattainable goals.

If many of these characteristics are present in an individual, according to Olivia Niehouse (1984), the individual may experience "job boredom, cynicism, unfulfilled need for recognition, moodiness, poor concentration, forgetfulness, and certain physical manifestations, such as stomach disorders and backache."

If these symptoms are present in individuals in an organization, both lost productivity and an increase in medical benefits used will occur. The organization can help. The biggest assistance is in the form of prevention programs, programs designed to reduce stress and help individuals set realistic career goals. This requires recognition on the part of the individual that a problem exists, which is also addressed in the employee assistance programs.

TAKING STEPS TO HANDLE STRESS AND BURNOUT

Once the difficulty is identified, individuals can begin to correct the situation by getting a realistic understanding of their career potential. This means the organization must provide excellent career counseling, either by an internal person or an external consultant. Again, the object is to provide an accurate assessment of the individual's career potential in the organization and the actual path or identity as soon as possible that maybe another organization would better fit the individual's career aspirations and abilities.

Second, every individual should begin to set attainable goals. Many individuals do not set goals for themselves or develop a plan of action to follow. In the Lewis Carroll story, *Alice's Adventures in Wonderland,* Alice asks which road at the fork she should take, but when she adds that she doesn't know where she wants to go, the Cheshire Cat says that either road will get her there. The moral of the story is that, without a plan, people may simply flounder. And in many careers, this floundering causes undue stress.

One needs to find a means of reducing the stress associated with the problems encountered in career decisions. Many techniques are available to reduce stress. One thing to keep in mind is that the successful application of these techniques is often based on the individual's commitment to making the needed changes and accurate identification of the causes of the stress. People also need to "face their problems calmly and rationally." As stated earlier, negative thinking only makes matter worse. Facing a stressful situation requires focusing all of your energy on the problem.

Also, many inexpensive biofeedback instruments that can provide quick insight into how to reduce stress levels can be purchased in most bookstores (Glicken 1985). For example, taking a deep breath or envisioning a pleasant scene can, in many cases, reduce the stress. There are also medically controlled chemical ways to reduce stress, which should probably be used only as a last resort, since other problems, including chemical addiction, could result.

In summary, individuals should be encouraged to take more control of their lives and their activities. Understanding personal and career objectives can lead to a higher quality of life. In some cases, people need help and many progressive organizations are offering this help through their employee assistance programs.

EMPLOYEE ASSISTANCE PROGRAMS

The philosophy behind the employee assistance programs (EAP) is to provide confidential, preventive assistance to employees and their families. The concept is built on the premise that employees' work-related or family-related problems will eventually result in job performance problems. In the past, companies simply took employees with problems through the disciplinary process in the hope that might solve the performance problems. Unfortunately, this approach usually resulted in termination of the employee. Clearly, this was difficult for the employees involved, probably had a negative effect on the morale of other employees, and resulted in a loss to the company of its investment in that individual.

After going through this process many times, companies became aware that they were discharging employees in whom the company had invested significant amounts of money to train and develop into fully functioning, productive workers. Accordingly, companies began searching for ways to help the employees with their problems and retain their investment in a fully qualified productive worker. Employee assistance programs have helped to fill the bill. They offer another mode of enhancing employee productivity and receiving the high investment return possible when the workforce is carefully managed.

History of Employee Assistance Programs

The first employee assistance program (EAP) in corporate America began at the E.I. duPont Company and focused on assisting employees who were experiencing alcohol-related problems. This idea became quite popular and was quickly copied by Eastman Kodak, Kemper Insurance, and Consolidated Edison (American Psychological Association 1985). As these programs grew, so too did the realization that employee problems involved more than alcohol-related problems. Five major areas where people have severe problems that will affect their performance on the job include alcohol, drugs, marital difficulties, legal difficulties, and financial difficulties. Considering the possible impact these problems can have on an individual's life, it is easy to understand how an individual's concentration could be diverted from work. Consider also that employees often experience more than one of the problems mentioned above at any given time. The synergistic impact of

FIGURE 5.2. Cartoon

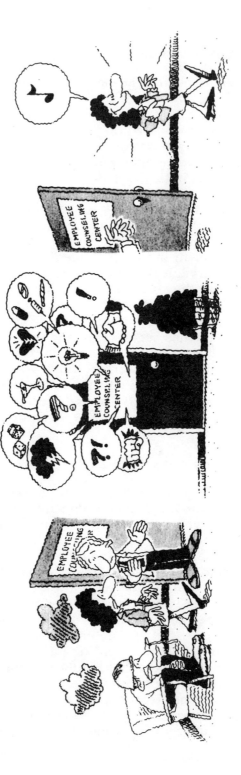

Source: Drawings by Spyder Webb. Reprinted with permission.

of this certainly takes its toll on the individual, the individual's performance, and, ultimately, the company.

Unrealized Cost of Problem Employees

There is ample evidence that employee problems lead to loss of productivity. According to Beinecke (1984), approximately 18 percent of the workforce is functioning at 75 percent of the average individual's productivity. This means that a company with 5,000 employees earning an average of $30,000 would be sustaining a productivity loss of 6.75 million dollars. That 6.75 million dollars is a reflection of problems associated with 900 employees (18 percent of 5,000). This figure is only the tip of the iceberg. There are many costs that are not seen on the bottom line results, but which do affect financial well-being. These can be broken into four main areas: personal costs, health care costs, hidden costs, and additional costs to industry. A summary of these costs is listed in Figure 5.3.

Alcohol abuse alone costs U.S. companies approximately $21 billion a year. Drug abuse alone costs another $17 billion, and other stress-related problems cost another $20 billion.

FIGURE 5.3. Unrealized Costs of Problem Employees

Personnel Costs
- Sick Leave Taken
- Absenteeism
- On the Job Accidents
- Leave Without Pay
- Absence Without Leave
- Suspension
- Replacement Costs
- Termination Costs

Health Care Costs
- Health Insurance Claims
- Sick Benefits Payments
- Accident Benefits Paid
- Outpatient Medical Visits
- Inpatient Medical Days
- Disability Retirement
- Worker's Compensation Claims

Hidden Costs
- Bad Business Decisions
- Diverted Supervisory Time
- Friction Among Workers
- Damage to Equipment
- Personnel Turnover
- Damage to Public Image

Additional Costs to Industry
- Discipline and Grievance Action
- Productivity Losses
- Corporate Theft
- Threat to Public Safety

Source: Richard H. Beinecke, "The Costs of Mental Health and Substance Abuse," Health Industries of America, One Report, January 19, 1984, pp. 25–26.

Adding about $80 billion spent on health insurance premiums, brings the cost to industry to approximately $138 billion (Beinecke 1984). That is a significant sum of money that results in a loss of productivity and clearly reflects poor use of resources—human resources and the money invested in them. This must be considered along with competition and other economic factors when evaluating difficulties experienced by industry today. Fortunately, EAPs can help. Results achieved by many organizations indicate that the money spent on implementing an EAP is money well spent. The U.S. Postal Service says that these programs have been worth $2 million to them, New York Telephone cites $1.5 million, and duPont claims a return on EAP investment of more than $500,000. For duPont, that translated to a $5.78 return for every dollar spent on EAP (American Psychological Association 1985). That is a return most companies would be proud to claim.

IMPLEMENTING EMPLOYEE ASSISTANCE PROGRAMS

While the costs are great and the returns from an EAP are good, implementing an EAP takes much effort. EAP is designed as a preventive measure. It looks at getting assistance for troubled employees before the problem becomes so large that it results in termination. While the process is effective for assisting troubled employees, its success does depend on employees making the contact. Help is available if the employee seeks it, but many are reluctant to seek it. This is one area of the program that can inhibit its overall success.

The EAP process, by design, attempts to eliminate this barrier. First of all, 24-hour, confidential access to help is provided for employees and, usually, their families. Knowing that they can get help when they need it, without incriminating themselves, is a necessity before an employee will make contact.

But what about the employees who do not recognize the problems or think that no help is needed? They may deny that a problem exists and they may also become extremely defensive when confronted about the issue. While this poses one of the greatest challenges for a supervisor, the EAP can make this confrontation more positive. First, problems experienced by individuals eventually surface at work, usually as a change in performance. What this performance change does is to give the superior something tangible with which to approach the employee—at this point to make the employee aware that a performance problem exists and that it must be corrected. The supervisor should avoid exploring any personal problems. To assist in the process of helping the employee, the supervisor should suggest that the EAP can help the individual if the individual feels that personal problems may be affecting work performance. The supervisor should reiterate that the EAP is a confidential process and that trained counselors are there to help the employee. In this case, the supervisor is offering the EAP as a means of help by referring the employee to someone skilled in dealing with the problems. Again, the supervisor is referring the employee to someone to seek help, not diagnosing the problem. For example, consider the following scenario (Scenario #1):

Supervisor: John, your drinking is causing me a problem. Get some help soon or you're fired.

Employee: I don't know what you're talking about. Sure, I have a few drinks to unwind at night, but that's all. I have no idea what you mean.

Supervisor: John, you know exactly what I mean. I'm not going to tolerate one more day of it. The next time, you're gone.

Nothing positive has been accomplished here. John knows the supervisor is mad at him, but may or may not be able or willing to change. John might not know what to change. John's denial that there is a problem suggests that the supervisor has done little to help clarify his problem. In addition, the supervisor is not a counselor and is not qualified to diagnose the problem. Obviously, calling an employee a drunkard is not an effective way to help an employee. Consider Scenario #2:

Supervisor: John, my records indicate you've been absent every Monday for the past three months. You know, John, when you're out on a Monday, it throws all of us out of schedule. Now, John, you know we talked about your absenteeism before. You told me you would change, but you continue to be absent. Now, John, you've been a good employee and I'd hate to lose you, but I cannot keep an employee who is absent frequently. It appears to me from my records that this frequent absenteeism started about four months ago. Now, John, I know this is not like you, and I think something is bothering you. I'd like to help you get some help.

Employee: What can I do? I don't want to lose my job, but I've got some problems at home that are getting the best of me!

Supervisor: John, I can understand how it must be when one experiences problems at home. And you know, John, it may seem overwhelming, but I think I've got something to help you. You know this company has an employee assistance program to help people such as you with problems. I recommend you call them immediately. They can help.

This interaction is more likely to have a positive outcome. The employee was confronted with facts. He was missing too much work. The fact was the employee's absenteeism was causing a problem to the company. This supervisor also exhibited empathy. He did not attack the employee personally. He attacked the employee's behavior—absenteeism. The problem and its implications were explained to the employee. In Scenario #2, the supervisor got involved, but without overstepping the boss/subordinate boundary.

Unfortunately, the techniques employed in Scenario #2 do not always work. No matter how hard a supervisor tries, the employee may not respond. In these instances, the supervisor must be firm, lay out the implications, and follow through. If an employee fails to get help, then the supervisor's only alternative may be to take the employee through the disciplinary process. Also note that going through the EAP does not exclude the possibility that the employee may also have to go through the disciplinary process. This would diminish the effectiveness of both the EAP and the organization's disciplinary process.

Once the employee is in the EAP, the EAP counselor begins to identify or diagnose the problem with the employee. Once this is done, steps to correct the problem are implemented. Because of the variety of problems encountered, it is impossible to identify a rigid step-by-step process. However, it is safe to say that the EAP counselors help in diagnosing the problem, counsel the employee, and try to treat the problem. In those instances where the problem warrants outside help, the EAP counselor arranges for that. For instance, if the problem is substance abuse, the EAP counselor may have the employee admitted to a hospital designed to overcome the addiction. In any case, the EAP is designed to solve the problem.

SUMMARY

In this chapter, stress has been considered in its broadest terms, defined, and discussed in terms of how the individual's perception of events can manifest stress.

The effect of stress on employee performance and the attendant effect on productivity is also examined. Clearly, lost productivity has a major impact on industry's "bottom line." Industry must address stress-related issues within the workforce in order to ensure that it maximizes use of its investment in that workforce and avoids the wastes that result from massive losses in productivity.

Use of employee assistance programs is considered. These are designed to help employees reduce stress through helping them to identify and work toward solving their problems. There is evidence that this approach will help to reduce poor work performance and will have a positive effect on employee productivity. Of course, the maintenance of well-trained, productive employees in the work force has a direct effect on industry's "bottom line." It is at least as important to keep human resources in good repair as it is to keep machines in good repair or other investments healthy and sound. The growth of employee assistance programs in the 1980s attests to the popularity and usefulness of this program.

6 Counseling: We Get By With A Little Help From Our Friends

INTRODUCTION

Between 10 and 20 percent of the labor force will utilize the services of a counselor in any one year (Holoviak and Holoviak 1984). The kind of counseling service may vary from a mental health service clinic to private psychiatrists/psychologists, trained ministers, and organization sponsored programs. When the topic of the counseling session is behavior and social adjustment, it is estimated that half of the problems identified in the sessions are related to problems reflected in the work environment. This results in troubled workers. These troubled workers have higher grievance rates, are involved in four times the number of accidents, use three times the normal sick leave days, and have the poorest record in absenteeism and turnover (Holoviak and Holoviak 1984).

Unfortunately, a great deal of time may pass before serious problems are identified without counseling, and by then it may be too late for meaningful corrective action. During this time, the organization feels the effects of impaired production, job mistakes, accidents, tardiness, and also absenteeism. If troubled workers are discharged, then the organization must retrain new employees and suffer the problems encountered with turnover (Rostain 1980).

For years industry and government employers have tried various techniques to cure the problems created by troubled workers. To control absenteeism, the traditional measures have concentrated on progressive discipline and punitive techniques. The results have been less than impressive. In reporting the results of such attempts, a Ford Motor Company representative indicated that the problem continued to increase (Robins 1979). Three of the largest farm equipment manufacturers tried using bonus programs for better attendance and tardiness records. They noted temporary improvements before employees reverted back to the prior poor record (Casio 1982). Some organizations are trying job enrichment to correct this problem. While this offers some promise, the conclusion is that, by itself, it will not be sufficient. For that matter, it is believed, no single program will suffice. Existing programs must be combined with something else (Casio 1982).

Counseling may be the program that will prove successful when combined with other organization efforts. The problems employees bring to the job include marital and family, mid-life stress, alcoholism, drug abuse, depression, and debt, to name a few. Conversely, many times the stress of one's job can affect life away from work. In addition, there are the intraorganizational matters of work environment stress associated with union/management relationships. This is especially likely if there is a hostile environment between the parties. Counseling may provide a vehicle to reduce problems at all these levels:

1) problems employees bring to work;
2) problems of work that affect life outside the organization; and
3) intraorganizational matters.

HISTORICAL USE OF COUNSELING

Organizations have become increasingly aware and interested in counseling as a tool, but the fact remains that programs are few in number and most are in the infancy stage of development. Among the Fortune 500 Companies, it is reported that fewer than 80 have counseling programs. Among this group, General Motors has one of the most extensive employee counseling programs (Collier and Landen 1978). There are records of the use of counseling programs as early as 1914, when the Ford Motor Company developed a program to advise employees on personal and legal matters. Macy's Department Store has employed a full-time psychiatrist since 1925 to help employees with both personal and work-related concerns (Dickeson and Roethlesberger 1966). The most extensive of all the early industrial counseling programs took place at the Western Electric Hawthorne Plant as a result of the Hawthorne studies. This program employed more than 50 counselors between 1936 and 1955 and included 20,000 counseling interviews (Holoviak and Holoviak 1984). The program instituted at the Western Electric Hawthorne Plant has served as a model for many of the counseling programs established during the 1960s and after.

DO PRACTITIONERS FEEL A NEED FOR COUNSELING?

For a relatively new concept to be successfully implemented, there must be awareness of its availability and desire of end users to actually want programs related to the concept. Available data suggest that practitioners in this area of expertise (i.e., personnel, labor relations, et cetera) are aware of counseling as an available tool. The extent to which their knowledge has been translated into practical applications is more difficult to uncover.

Research on the use of counseling indicates that psychologists, psychiatrists, and psychiatric social workers, not in-house counselors or personnel managers, are delivering the service (Cristiani and Cristiani 1979).

In a research study conducted using random sample among members of the American Society of Personnel Administrators

TABLE 6.1. Areas Where Personnel/Labor Relations Specialists Need Training

Unprepared Areas	Number Responding	Percent	Rank
Affirmative action	40	52	1
Discriminatory practices	36	47	2
Employee alcoholism	35	46	3
Employee discrimination	35	46	3
Comparable worth	34	44	5
Employee drug abuse	31	40	6
Developing pay levels	30	39	7
Employee counseling	29	38	8
Career development & counseling	28	36	9
Communications	27	35	10
Employee dishonesty	26	34	11
Employee formal complaints	24	31	12
Occupational safety and health administration issues	24	31	12
Employee motivation	22	29	14
Training practices	21	27	15
Employee morale	19	25	16
Quotas	16	21	17
Employee absenteeism	16	21	17
Employee turnover	12	16	19
Recruitment	11	14	20

Source: *Performance and Instruction 24*, No. 3 (April 1985): 1. Reprinted with permission.

(ASPA), 38 percent of the respondents indicated that counseling was an area where they would desire training. Of the list of 20 items, ASPA members were asked to prioritize for themselves the importance of each in training. Counseling ranked eighth on the list (Holoviak, DeCenzo, and Holoviak 1985).

Among the rankings, it is important to note that several items are frequently handled by counseling methods. Employee alcoholism, drug abuse, and career development ranked third, sixth, and ninth, respectively.

Another aspect of this research study dealt with overall objectives to be met by training in the field of personnel/labor relations. As indicated in Table 6.2, the second ranked item was for training in the area of understanding the concerns of employees and being skilled in handling problems. This grouping has as its main ingredients counseling techniques for use by staff personnel/labor relations employees (Holoviak, et. al. 1985).

The research implied a strong need for training of staff personnel/labor relations employees. It should be noted that other research suggests that counseling should not be undertaken without the proper training. These results show a difference in results between trained and untrained counselors ("Personnel's Newest Service" 1978). Where the counseling was utilized with-

TABLE 6.2. Objectives to be Met by Offering Personnel/Labor Relations Training

Objectives	Number Responding	Percent	Rank
The initial job skills of the personnel/labor relations person	60	78	3
Philosophical knowledge of personnel management/ labor relations	58	75	4
Understanding employee concerns/skills in handling problems	63	82	2
Narrow specialization areas	43	56	5
Broad knowledge of personnel management/ labor relations	73	95	1

Source: *Performance and Instruction 24*, No. 3 (April 1985): 2. Reprinted with permission.

out the proper skills training, low ratings with regard to the success in handling of problems were received.

WILL EMPLOYEES ACCEPT COUNSELING?

From the above discussion, it appears that practitioners in the field have a desire to utilize counseling to handle employee-related problems successfully. Historically, there are indicators of program use over seventy years ago. The literature suggests that the composition of the workforce has changed over the past decades. This change occurred in education levels, attitudes toward work, leisure time preferences, job fulfillment, and the like. Will the contemporary employee be accepting of counseling programs? In 1978 a survey was carried out with 2,000 workers to evaluate their feedback to the idea of counseling. From the research, several points emerged to support the use of counseling (Finkelstein and Ziegenfuss 1978).

The first point to emerge was that one-third of the sample group of employees said they would utilize the help of counseling on a wide variety of topics. Second, over 26 percent of the respondents knew a fellow worker who had missed work due to a problem, and 27 percent knew of employees whose work was hindered because of problems. Third, 58 percent indicated a desire for such a program to be in-house in the organization, and approximately 47 percent felt the organization should handle the cost of the program (Finkelstein and Ziegenfuss 1978).

WHERE COUNSELING CAN BE USED

For many practitioners, if counselors handled only absenteeism and alcoholism problems with some degree of success, they would feel the program had paid for itself. Figures indicate that, nationally, employee absenteeism costs workers and our economy $20 billion a year in lost pay, and costs their organizations $10 billion in sick pay and $5 billion in fringe benefits that continue despite the absence of the employee (Casio 1982). The cost of alcoholism and drug abuse is estimated to reach $75 billion annually (Miles 1985). Research also indicates that one in 10 employees is an alcoholic and one in 20 has a drug problem (Miles 1985). Some other findings on alcoholic workers only reinforce the need to provide corrective action. Some of these findings for alcoholic workers include:

1) They are 2.5 times as likely to be absent as other workers.
2) Their accident rate is 3.6 times the normal.
3) They use three times the amount of sick leave usually. required.
4) They cost significantly more in extras for such items as ruined materials, wasted time, et cetera (Milbourn 1984).

As significant as the above figures are, it is also important to stress that many of the costs of absenteeism and alcoholism are covered up in a variety of production and accounting data that make it hard to know the true magnitude of the problem (Casio 1982).

Beyond the two serious problems indicated above, counseling services are responding to accidents, career path development, legal matters, marital problems, retirement, relocation, job transfers, as well as stress resulting from skills becoming obsolete due to rapidly changing technology. In some instances, industrial counselors may be asked to advise on corporate policies, educate management on matters of mental health, and aid in the design of psychologically healthy working conditions.

In a slightly different approach from directly addressing employee personal problems, some counselors are asked to look at the interpersonal problems of employees. In some cases they focus on both the individual and the work environment. These specialists study human factors in production output in an attempt to develop working conditions that will emphasize output by focusing on personal strengths and deemphasizing personal weaknesses or facilities (Feingold 1971).

Many counselors have tried to avoid this form of counseling. Yet increasingly, they are asked to examine work place problems, problems of organization inefficiency, worker empathy, incompetency, destructive intergroup competition, and other forms of conflict (Leonard 1977).

To help with the problems of intraorganizational adversarial problems between unions and management, counselors can serve as a communication channel between employee, union, and employer. This is carried out without the unpleasant conditions that are attached to industrial spying.

Besides being helpful in aiding supervisor-employee, union-employee, and employee-management relations, the industrial counseling program has been valuable in improving the personal adjustment of individual employees. This has the benefit of reducing job stress factors that affect life away from work. The industrial counselor can be useful in helping increase positive employee attitudes because these counselors are in a position that enables them to promote group cooperation and to help the employee visualize the goal. They can also help the employees adjust toward the meaning of their work in relationship to achieving the goal.

In helping an employee adjust to work, a question that rises is how often and to what extent should an employee be counseled. One argument is that counseling should take place only in cases of declines in worker output, the other is that counseling should be conducted on some regular schedule. A compromise approach to the above extremes utilizes the organization grievance (complaint handling) mechanisms and the supervisor to handle routine and job-related problems, and refers more serious, complex, or personal problems to the counselor.

General Motors Corporation employs between 75 and 100 professionals to deal with problems associated with absenteeism, alcoholism, careless workmanship, as well as with feelings of withdrawal or anger against the company (Collier and Landen 1978).

FORMAT FOR DELIVERY OF COUNSELING SERVICE

As would be suspected, there are various formats for delivery of counseling services. The scenarios range from basic referrals to outside services to complex in-house systems staffed by psychiatrists and counselors, to training by psychologists on behavior modification to handle employee problems.

Outside Agencies

As an outgrowth of the drug scare in the 1960s, various services arose to help people with drug problems. Some companies took advantage of this and either referred employees, made the service available at no cost to the employee, or simply acted as an information conduit of the service availability. One small Kansas City organization took advantage of such a service. The organization employed 200 in five U.S. cities. From 1975 to 1978 it was estimated that three-fourths of the staff had used the services, which was credited in helping the employees become more productive and catch problems before formal complaints arose ("Personnel's Newest Service" 1978).

In addition, many communities have programs open to the public that deal with a wide variety of problems. While research suggests these may not be as successful as in-house programs, there are records of positive results from their utilization. For example, the Employee Counseling Service in New York City is one of the largest of its kind in the country. One New York agency credited its use with saving $27,000 due to reduced absenteeism as 51 employees participated in a six-month program (Rostain 1980).

Management has also used clergy as counselors. The fact that clergy may be attractive to employees as well as not prohibitively costly to employers has made this alternative attractive.

Behavior Modification Training

Behavior modification training is a technique to teach managers how to handle employee problems in a positive manner using the latest state of the art skills. For example, these were used at the Pacific and the Illinois divisions of the Bell Company. Two groups were used, a test group trained in behavior modification skills and the control group, which was not trained. After the training, the supervisors in both groups were evaluated as to solutions to three separate problems presented to them. Results showed that 82 percent of the Illinois and 86 percent of the Pacific groups who had received training were evaluated on their handling the sample situations in an above-average manner, with many of the supervisors handling the sample situations in an excellent fashion. For the group not trained in behavior modification techniques, 30 percent in each division were felt to have handled the problems in a below-average fashion. Handling in a below-average fashion for the trained people compares to two percent of the Pacific group and nine percent of the trained group in Illinois. This information helps demonstrate the need for training if staff persons are expected to handle problems in lieu of trained counselors ("Personnel's Newest Service" 1978).

In-House Programs

In-house programs appear from research that has been conducted to be the preferred format. In-house means trained counselors are part of the staff of employees, not trained personnel/labor relations staff. That is, unless the training is to such an extent as to qualify them as a counselor. Throughout the chapter, in-house programs have been cited. They are used with General Motors Corporation, Western Electric, Ford Motor Corporation, Macy's Department Store, and approximately 80 of the Fortune 500 companies.

THE COUNSELING PROCESS

Whether it is done in-house or at an outside agency, the counseling process by a trained counselor is basically the same. That is, the person must move through various stages in the process to achieve a behavioral shift.

Depending on the theoretical training of the counselor, this can vary from two to six stages or steps. The different theories may condense or expand upon a particular point in the process, but all have the prerequisite that for movement to the next stage, the goals of the current stage must be accomplished (Blackham 1977). The point of the discussion here is not to turn the reader into a counselor with a short description, but to inform the reader about the process. The particular activities and tasks involved in the therapy will vary depending on the nature of the employee problem.

The counseling process described here will be a four stage movement: 1) problem identification and establish relationship, 2) explanation and analysis, 3) implementation, and 4) ending the process (Blackham 1977). We will look at the basic elements in each part to give a flavor for the process.

Problem Identification and Establishing a Relationship

Much of the first-stage work takes place during the first session. The counselor will concentrate on several main objectives (Blackham 1977). First is to develop a helping relationship. The mutual contact of an interview is important to set the stage for what follows in subsequent sessions. During this point, clients may not divulge the "real" reason they are seeing the counselor, but will give what sounds like an acceptable answer.

The second objective is to assist employees to state any fears, concerns, problems, or why they feel they need help. The third objective is to determine the extent to which help can be offered. This involves defining the structure and conditions under which help will be offered. It may mean the necessity to include others in the session, or referral to a specialized agency, depending on the problem.

Explanation and Analysis

This stage involves a significant amount of client analysis. Conditions are fostered that help the employees visualize and understand the nature of their difficulties. From this an action plan is devised to solve the problems. This stage involves four key objectives. First is to detail the employee difficulty on behavioral terms so that it becomes possible to find solutions. These should be within parameters of employee-oriented behavior that can be learned (taught) and/or changed and within the realities of the person's lifestyle. Second, each of the problems must be broken down into the various components (variables) that caused the problem to exist and any factors that cause the problems to continue at the current level. Third, the problems are prioritized. Last, conditions that can reduce the problem variables and help the employee to solve the problem are explored.

Implementation

This is an active problem-solving environment. New behaviors are learned, reinforced if they are the desired ones, and decisions are made for plans that will develop into positive action. During this stage the counselor is in honest communication with the employee. Regular feedback is given to the employee to show understanding, empathy, and to encourage corrective results and actions.

Ending the Process

If the process laid out in the first three steps has been realistic, and each step worked through with the employee, ending the relationship is a natural step. Occasionally the time limits for completion of goals goes beyond reasonable measure. In these cases the counselor and employee review the process, procedures for modification, and consider the possibility of referral to another counselor.

Termination does not indicate the counselor is no longer interested in the employee. Within the industrial setting, problem employees will continue to be evaluated and follow-up sessions with employees are desired to ensure continuity of procedure. Furthermore, the employee has the comfort of knowing that future assistance is available if needed.

COUNSELING AS A MANAGERIAL STRATEGY

From the general discussion indicated in this chapter and by intuitive reasoning, the fewer the problems the employees have to deal with the better they can do their jobs. Counseling is a vehicle to address these and keep the impact on the job to as small as possible. Several writers in the field believe that counseling philosophy should be implemented as a managerial strategy. It is perceived that counseling is an integral managerial function not only as a technique for remedying individual problems of employee mental health, but in fostering a deliberate creation of a pleasant organization which will have increased production efficiency and reduced adversarial climate.

SUMMARY

With the growth in research and training into the area of counseling, this tool is emerging as a real possibility for managers to utilize. One only needs to look to the rising numbers using the service to feel that there is acceptance of the process across all levels of society.

The tremendous cost associated with employees who face alcohol- and drug-related problems further serves to emphasize the need to sharpen skills or to bring trained counselors into the organization as part of the team. Recent research discussed in this chapter reveals the desires of human resource (both personnel and labor relations staff) people to receive more training in this area, and to utilize counselors.

The utilization is to include areas such as alcohol and drug abuse. But, as indicated, the possibilities go much further. That is, it offers positive approaches to absenteeism, tardiness, turnover, job burnout, career development, and other direct career-related issues. Furthermore, its potential encompasses areas of personal problems that keep employees from performing in an efficient and cost-effective mode: stress reduction, marital counseling, how to handle troubled children, family planning, "getting over" a divorce, future retirement, and much more. The key point is that counseling is a proactive technique management can use to protect and enhance its valuable investment in its human resources.

III   Taking Care of Business: Costing It and Writing It

Part III looks in depth at the technical side of the labor relations process. It brings to surface the latest research and thought on the topics and offers guidance in making the technical side of the process work better.

Technical guidance and new points of sophistication are offered in how to cost and negotiate a labor contract. This includes a whole chapter, Chapter 9, on handling the expensive and sensitive area of benefits. Chapter 10 concentrates on writing the agreement. Writing to avoid ambiguities and to ensure that the end user, not just the corporate counsel, can understand and use the final result is of obvious importance. Suggestions in this area are included.

Chapters 11 and 12 work on corrective action and formal arbitration. By the very nature of the management-labor relationship process in the U.S., there have historically been adversarial situations. The authors attempt to demonstrate that corrective action can be positive, leading to worker improvement, and that the arbitration process can be more professional and effective.

7 Where The Bargaining Process Currently Stands

INTRODUCTION

Economic conditions, especially the combined past effects of recession, inflation, and high interest rates, have magnified the importance of even the smallest benefit decisions made during collective bargaining negotiations—for both union and company negotiators and for the people they represent.

Changes in wage rates and productivity relative to principal trading nations of the United States have been a source of concern for both labor and management. Productivity statistics are no more optimistic, with the productivity of the United States' principal training nations increasing at a greater rate than that of the United States. In addition, management has had to confront the reality of rising benefit costs and the fact that the returns to their companies for benefit outlays tend to be low.

Unfortunately, the problems and concerns that face labor and management have been compounded by the fact that companies and unions have both failed to perform in-depth cost analyses of the benefits packages. All of the above problems and concerns are brought to the negotiating table.

In the past, much of the difficulty encountered in reaching effective agreements has stemmed from misunderstandings and misperceptions on the part of all involved. These are due, in large measure, to the failure of unions and companies to perform in-depth cost analyses of contract agreements. This failure results in an inability to develop and communicate accurate and reliable figures, which means labor and management cannot reach a mutual understanding of the value of the agreement and its long-range economic effects on both parties.

It is essential that appropriate guidelines be established to refine skill levels of practitioners and students in the field of human resource management, especially those that apply to the areas of labor relations and collective bargaining. These guidelines require an integration of accounting, financial analysis, and labor relations principles in order to be effective in meeting the increasingly complex needs of negotiators at the collective bargaining table. The objective of this chapter and Chapters 8 and 9 will be to provide these necessary guidelines. This chapter will include a brief outline of where the beginning process currently stands.

HOW MANAGEMENT AND LABOR ORGANIZE THEMSELVES FOR BARGAINING

Companies organize their personnel and labor relations functions in different ways. Areas of responsibility for personnel and labor relations differ. Some companies may place the responsibility for the labor relations function at the corporate vice-presidential level, while others place it at the middle-management level.

As students and practitioners of labor relations are aware, location in the hierarchy coupled with commensurate authority of the labor staff person is important. The individual's location can affect the overall quality and effectiveness of labor-management relations for the company. Theory notes that a staff person should be located as near the operating site as possible with authority to settle labor disputes or problems that arise. This individual could have line authority over this situation.

There is little agreement in the literature regarding whether the collective bargaining function should be centralized or decentralized, although there is some indication that the decentralized model of authority can result in more productive operations. Unfortunately, there is also some evidence that U.S. collective bargaining systems may not be constructed along the lines of the more efficient model.

Union structure for collective bargaining appears to be reactive in nature; that is, its structure seems to flow in response to how companies organize for collective bargaining. Following the assumption in the above discussion that the collective bargaining model most widely used in U.S. firms is a highly centralized one, the move to centralized bargaining structures by unions over the past 20 years can be more easily understood. This has been done in many cases to balance the power of the companies.

Union negotiators are vested with authority to make key decisions only to the extent they feel the membership will support these decisions. In cases where there has been contact among leaders from the international, the local, and the rank-and-file, and when the membership is satisfied with its leadership, ratification of the contract becomes more certain.

While more centralized responsibility for negotiations is generally characteristic of union negotiations, lack of support from the international staff or the field representative need not spell defeat for the local negotiator. The local can present a strong and professional showing at the bargaining table through using some basic costing techniques and other available resources.

In summary, it should be noted that while both companies and unions currently have centralized organizations for collective bargaining negotiations, they are moving toward more decentralized organization. Skills, responsiblity, and authority are not necessarily found in any one person, much less the person doing the negotiating. Ideally, both union and company negotiators would have the necessary skills and authority to negotiate effectively, backed up by informed and integrated contract-costing preparation by support staffs at a more centralized level.

KEY PROBLEMS IN EXISTING NEGOTIATING PROCEDURES

One key problem in existing negotiating procedures is that the people in charge of negotiations fail to utilize fully the wide assortment of technically skilled help available to them (Granof 1973). Available help includes experts from the accounting, finance, compensation, personnel, and planning departments.

Another reason that contract costing and other financial and planning aspects of labor relations are relatively inefficient is that they often fail to get enough data to work with or fail to use the correct types of data. Most companies prepare long-range plans that indicate anticipated volume, price, and capital investment; however, most cost calculations for contract preparations are limited to historical data.

In addition, labor contract analysts and negotiators tend to disregard the effects of their decisions on other functional areas of company operations. This could be a result of limited information from other departments or of insufficient skills to complete the analysis.

ROLE OF COMPUTERS

With all the complexities involved in costing a labor contract, it is natural to assume that computers have been used extensively in the approximately 193,000 agreements that are in effect. In reality, few companies or unions have applied the sophisticated computer-aided mathematical techniques used elsewhere in organizations for costing anticipated union demands.

Any computer application for many of the problems encountered in the collective bargaining process is still theoretical. This is due to the loosely structured nature of labor relations problems. Yet, computer applications for costing contract demands is quite feasible.

Much of the problem in using computers rests with the fact that companies and unions fail to implement a comprehensive recordkeeping system. For example EDP records of data on absenteeism may record only the person's time away from the job. Yet, to record the cost properly, the record should include data regarding allowances for replacement personnel and any deviations in output resulting from the absenteeism of the more skilled person.

Use of computers is widely accepted in personnel areas, but the records need to be improved so they include a broader body of information. Future computer applications depend on adequate data bases from which to make complete cost analyses. The potential for use of computers in collective bargaining is vast. Applications in the current state of the art are

1) analysis of past contract cost estimates relative to their actual cost;
2) costing alternative package proposals during negotiations; and
3) analyzing contract demands and their effect on wage rate, product price, productivity, and profit levels.

REVERSE COLLECTIVE BARGAINING

Reverse collective bargaining, or the concession of labor to management requests for "give-backs" of wages or benefits agreed upon in previous contract negotiations, must be considered in any discussion of collective bargaining.

The goal of negotiations from the union perspective since the beginning of the labor movement in the 1930s has been to gain more for its constituency in terms of wages and benefits. Recently, however, labor has been willing to grant give-backs to management if the company's ability to stay in business might be jeopardized by a disproportionate wage and benefit burden. Concessions can take the form of actual decreases in wages or benefits, wage or benefit freezes, sharply curtailed wage or benefit increases, or an end to restrictive work rules that reduce management's flexibility in assignment of workers.

An example of a positive reverse bargaining negotiation is the case of the Teamsters in 1981–82. They believed negotiations of this kind were needed to help the transportation industry. In fact, the Teamsters opened talks before the expiration of the existing agreements in the hope that they could help the ailing truck companies with problems arising from industry deregulation.

While unions have generally resisted the reverse collective bargaining movement, there are hundreds of cases of concessions granted in recent negotiations. It should be noted that the granting of concessions is not a phenomenon unique to this current economic period. Cases include: the Aluminum Workers granting concessions to Aliva at Chillicothe, Ohio; the International Union of Electricians granting concessions to General Motors' Frigidaire plant at Dayton, Ohio, and Sylvania at Batavia, New York; and the United Auto Workers granting concessions to Chrysler Corporation, among others (Henle, 1973).

The reverse collective bargaining process is not only time-consuming but also highly sensitive. The process requires careful and comprehensive planning, an atmosphere of mutual good faith between labor and management, political savvy and understanding, and effective handling of the complex variables involved.

Trouble areas that have arisen in this process include subsequent actions taken on the part of management that jeopardize its credibility with labor. Examples of these actions include salary increases, bonuses, or other forms of excess paid to the managerial staff; situations in which the company experiences excess profits and makes no move to recognize the worker's contribution and sacrifice; and senior management taking the situation for granted and assuming that once reverse collective bargaining has been used, it will always be available.

Politically difficult situations that arise in subsequent negotiations stemming from establishing precedents in seemingly similar, yet actually different situations may also present trouble. These situations often occur when a local union deals with several companies. In that case, the union may receive complaints that the concessions to one company place other companies at a competitive disadvantage. Another politically difficult situation arises when competing unions try to take over representation of the workers by claiming that the current union representative's having given concessions proves the weakness of the representative in serving its membership.

In summary, reverse collective bargaining can be an important tool for assuring that businesses survive, thereby saving worker's jobs. However, it requires careful planning, negotiations based on mutual trust and actual needs, and responsible follow-through on the part of both labor and management. It should be noted that there are very few cases where only labor's concessions have been of help to the company in trouble. To salvage a troubled company requires concessions and cooperation from both labor and management.

SUMMARY

This chapter has been designed to help the reader gain insight into the current status of collective bargaining in the United States.

There are two interdependent points of view that must be examined. Wages, representing labor's point of view, and productivity, representing management's point of view, are both increasing at a slower rate in the U.S. than in its principal trading nations. It is not hard to understand, with that in mind, that benefit costs to management and benefit value to workers are becoming increasingly important concerns. It is essential, therefore, that the benefit sections of collective bargaining agreements be developed effectively, in both short-and long-term perspective.

To deal effectively with these issues the practitioner should understand who is responsible for negotiations for both labor and management, how each group tends to be organized, and what problems each group faces in preparing for and carrying out the negotiating process.

In addition, the practitioner should be aware of the existing usefulness of computers and their huge potential for use in collective bargaining negotiations.

Also included in this chapter is a section on reverse collective bargaining, which, while certainly controversial, is being used in industry with increasing frequency.

Chapters 8 and 9 set forth a practical approach for developing and costing collective bargaining agreements that are mutually beneficial for both labor and management. This chapter and the following three chapters rely heavily on Steve Holoviak's book, *Costing Labor Contracts* (1984).

8 Costing Wage Requests

INTRODUCTION

Wages make up the largest part of the compensations package for most companies and must therefore be costed accurately. A 1979 Chamber of Commerce Survey reports that the average company pay breakdown, excluding benefits, included 93.7 percent for straight time, 3.6 percent for premium pay (overtime), 0.6 percent for holiday pay, 0.6 percent for shift differentials, 1.1 percent of incentive pay, and 0.4 percent for other items.

Wage-Productivity Debate

A problem of some concern to negotiators on both sides of the table has been that wage increases have outstripped productivity gains in recent years. The rate of change in productivity has varied considerably among industries recently. The Bureau of Labor Statistics notes that during the period from 1975 to 1980, three-fourths of reporting industries showed lower gains in productivity than were recorded between 1947 and 1975 (BLS Bulletin 2128, 1982). Nonfarm business productivity increased at a rate of 2.4 percent per year from 1947 to 1975, while the annual growth rate from 1975 to 1980 was only 0.6 percent (Bureau of Labor Statistics 1982).

On the other hand, compensation paid to employees has displayed a different trend, with recorded compensation increases across industries for the period from 1950 through 1975 averaging 5.4 percent and the average for the period from 1965 through 1975 averaging 9.0 percent.

For an even clearer picture of what has been happening, compensation trends can be compared with trends in output per man-hour. Indexed with 1967 = 100, and examining from that period to 1978, compensation has increased 8 percent per year between 1967 and 1978, while output has increased only 1.2 percent during the same period.

This chapter will present issues regarding costing of wages and various techniques for costing wages. Understanding the basic format will enable the negotiator to cost items not addressed specifically, contributing to a more effective and realistic exchange at the bargaining table.

Are Unions to Blame for Productivity Declines and Spiraling Wages?

Union negotiators use the evidence of increased worker output as justification for demanding higher wages. Their rationale is that if productivity is increasing, there must certainly be new and higher profits available from which the wages demanded can be paid. The assumption by union negotiators is that all other factors involved in production have remained the same and the increased productivity has resulted from labor contributions only. Unfortunately, management negotiators

TABLE 8.1. Index of Output and Wages Per Man-Hour, 1965 to 1978 (1967 = 100)

	Compensation per Man-Hour		Output per Man-Hour	
Year	Private Business Sector	Nonfarm Business Sector	Private Business Sector	Nonfarm Business Sector
1965	88.6	89.3	95.0	95.9
1970	123.1	121.7	104.2	103.1
1971	131.4	129.9	107.8	106.3
1972	139.7	138.3	111.4	110.1
1973	151.1	149.1	113.6	112.0
1974	164.8	162.7	110.1	108.5
1975	181.2	178.8	112.4	110.5
1976	197.0	193.7	116.4	114.4
1977	213.0	209.3	118.2	115.8
1978	232.7	228.7	118.6	116.4

Source: Productivity Indexes for Selected Industries, 1977 Edition, Bureau of Labor Statistics Bulletin 1983 (Washington, D.C.: U.S. Department of Labor, 1977).

are not always well equipped with answers based on principles of labor economics. For example, if new technology (capital) has been used to raise the output level, then the added income that results from the increased productivity may not be immediately available for distribution to labor or stockholders. For the company to experience continued growth in productivity, the cost of new technology must be accounted for and paid prior to raising wages (Rees 1959).

In the long-run analysis, the union negotiator's point of view that increases in productivity are the appropriate criteria against which wage increases should be weighed is correct. However, in the short-run, use of increased productivity as a direct measure of the appropriate increase in wages is not correct and will only prove harmful to the company's capability to achieve long-run profitability.

Studies show that union workers do in fact earn higher wages than their nonunion counterparts. H. Gregg Lewis conducted a comprehensive study of union/nonunion wage differences and found a relationship between the level of unionism and the wages union workers receive relative to nonunion workers. While the study is somewhat dated for current contract use, the correlation showed unionized workers receive between 10 to 15 percent higher wages (Lewis 1963).

Thomas Kochan (1980) summarized more recent results of the numerous other attempts to judge the impact of unions on wage rates. His findings suggest that unions appear to have a more positive effect on the wages of black males than those of white males, that the normal age/earning profile of the nonunion sector is leveled by unionization, thus reducing the influence of age and education on earnings, that union wage effects vary across occupations and industries, and that in firms where blue-collar workers are organized, unions reduce the white-collar/blue collar wage difference.

In addition, unionization leads to increased productivity. A host of studies have shown that unionized companies within the same industry, with other factors held equal, experience 6 to 30 percent greater productivity than their nonunionized counterparts (Oswald 1981). Furthermore, productivity in organized settings tends to be increased by a high enough amount to offset the increase in total costs of higher union wages (Freeman and Medoff 1979). These findings lend strong support to the union negotiator's viewpoint.

DETERMINANTS OF WAGES

Before investigating how to cost wage demands, a review of the basic determinants impacting on wage policy may prove helpful. It is extremely important to develop a strong awareness of the key factors that affect this highly sensitive worker issue—no other area of employment can cause greater emotional response than wage adjustments. The following delineation of these factors will help alleviate much of the confusion that has kept economists from being able to create effective predictive models in this area.

Area Wage Competition

Competition in the labor market clearly exists, making it necessary for any wage-determination model to allow for variations in local markets. Theory indicates that job worth, as identified through conducting a job analysis and job evaluation, is the criterion for wage determination. Yet market conditions, such as a shortage of workers in a needed skill category, may force a higher wage rate than technical analysis would suggest. People costing increases in this area for predictive purposes often use area market wage changes as the standard.

Company Policy

One example of how company policy can affect determination of wages would be following a practice of being a wage leader, that is, paying the highest wages in the local labor market area. This policy is based on the belief that higher productivity can be secured by attracting the best workers in each skill category, which can be accomplished by paying the highest wages. Theoretically, the increased productivity will offset the increased cost of wages. No empirical data currently exist to verify such an assumption.

Another variation of the company policy involves the desire to give employees real wage increases, that is increases beyond maintenance of purchasing power toward increased living standards. This philosophy is rather common among companies that are attempting to be socially responsible.

It should be kept in mind that the nature of increases tends to be decided through the typical give-and-take bargaining framework. In negotiation situations, the initial costing assumptions rely on economic data regarding cost-of-living changes and estimates from top management as to how much of a real wage increase is desired.

Ability to Pay

An obvious area of importance to the company and to the union is the company's ability to pay. Typically, in times of good sales and profits, little resistance is offered to upward wage and benefit adjustments. When sales and profits drop, management resists these adjustments on the premise that they are unable to pay. Union negotiators offer little argument when sales and profits are good, but can be caught in a serious dilemma when sales and profits are not good. One rationale union negotiators offer for their hesitation to support management's position on the down side is that if concessions in wages are granted to individual companies in a given industry, a competitive advantage is given to the inefficient company while the efficient ones are punished. Union negotiators, therefore, tend to maintain a strong position for uniformity.

There are better defenses against providing wage increases than relying on a generalized statement that the company is unable to pay. A more sophisticated, and potentially more effective, defense would include delineation of the specific areas the demand might impact unfairly, including

1) its effect on the capital-labor ratio;
2) changes necessary in product mix;
3) changes in price-volume relationships;
4) changes in productivity over the expected life of the demand; and
5) impact on nonbargaining unit employees.

The important thing to keep in mind is that the effects of a demand go beyond obvious areas. A change in wages, for example, could affect any or all of the above mentioned areas.

Other Determinants

The above determinants have a clearly defined relationship to wage and benefit changes. Other determinants do influence negotiations, but their effect is more difficult to measure. Many are in the area of labor economics. Product market influence and industry concentration on wage levels are two examples. Highly concentrated industries (those with a few companies) tend, for instance, to be associated with higher wage levels. There is much disagreement among labor economists regarding these factors and no definitive statements can be made. Therefore, it is acknowledged that other influences may exist; but the emphasis here is on those that can be more clearly defined.

BASIC COSTING TECHNIQUES

There are five commonly accepted basic techniques for costing wage and economic proposals (a combination of techniques may also be used):

1) Total annual cost, which is the total amount spent by a company over a period of time (usually a year) for a given benefit. This figure usually excludes any administrative costs.
2) Cost per employee per year, which is found by dividing the total cost of the benefits by some average number of workers over the time period in question or by the specific number of workers covered by that benefit.
3) Percent of the payroll, which is found for the particular benefit in question by dividing the total cost of providing the benefit by the total payroll. The figure to use for total payroll may include all payments to workers or all payments except overtime and shift differentials.
4) Cents per hour is the terminology used to describe the money requested by the union per hour per employee.
5) Cost per hour is found by dividing the total cost of the benefit by total productive hours worked by all employees in the time period.

In preparing for costing wage and economic proposals, it is necessary to gather certain information. A general listing of information that may be required appears in Figure 8.1. Note that not all categories will be needed for each of the five techniques.

Total Annual Cost

Knowing the total annual cost of a given benefit is valuable for budgeting, for justifying the existence of the benefit, and for describing the total outlays involved in a benefit program. Thanks to computerized accounting systems that can capture these data (which require only minor adjustments), this figure is relatively easy for most companies to obtain. Certain benefits such as pension, profit-sharing, and various insurance costs can be easily figured in this manner. Others may not be so easily figured. The true total cost for these other benefits

FIGURE 8.1. General Listing of Information Required to Compute the Cost of Economic Benefits

Number of full-time employees
Number of part-time permanent employees
Number of part-time temporary employees
Number of full-time equivalent employees
Distribution of employees by job title
Distribution of employees by pay grades
Distribution of employees by length of service
Distribution of employees by shift
Number of employees who work seven-day week
Number of employees who regularly work Saturday, Sunday, and holidays who are not seven-day workers
Distribution of employees by number of dependents

may not be readily available in the more traditional accounting systems. For example, employee discounts on merchandise may show only total discount figures taken, rather than the loss, profit, or added sales necessary to recoup the costs of the benefit.

Cost Per Employee Per Year

Finding the cost per employee per year for some benefits requires only simple accounting procedures. For example, figures on pay for time not worked, such as vacations and holiday pay, are especially simple to ascertain. Finding individual costs for group health plans and other benefits can be more difficult. These situations require that records of employee participation and the total cost to the company be maintained. From this information, the cost per employee can be obtained by dividing the cost figure by the number of workers participating. For the more easily accrued data where participation of all workers is mandatory, a simple division of cost by total workers will produce the desired figure.

Percent of Payroll

Once all benefit areas are identified and classified, the cost of each benefit category and its own cost as a percentage of total payroll is calculated. Note that careful recordkeeping is necessary for classifying and identifying benefits. In addition, certain key points should be remembered:

1) Shift differentials should be excluded from total cost figures subject to separate demands.
2) Any planned expansions or contractions of the workforce should be taken into account to adjust the total payroll figure, along with possible change in the "mix of new pay rates."
3) Planned changes in production processes resulting from new technology or equipment that would alter the workforce mix should be taken into account.
4) It is advantageous to determine the cost of a one percent wage change. This allows for ease in recomputation during bargaining as demands and counter offers are exchanged and altered.

The percent of payroll technique is the simplest way to figure the cost of a union request, provided it is made in percentage form (such as 5 percent or 10 percent increase for all covered workers). The percentage increase is found by multiplying total dollar payroll of covered workers by the percentage requested. Any planned changes from the current period, such as a change in the number of workers, should be figured into the calculations. Major policy decisions, such as what is to be included as payroll cost, must be made by company management when costing by this technique. Some companies include only straight-time cost, while others include straight time plus any bonus income to be used in computing certain future benefits, such as pensions.

Firms frequently find it advantageous to figure the cost of a 1 percent change in any benefits or wages as a guide for use in contract negotiations. This permits quick and easy computation and recomputation during the negotiation sessions (Heisel and Skinner 1976).

Cents Per Hour

Often, union demands for wage increases will be for a certain number of cents per hour to be added to the basic pay rate of each employee. If there are no planned changes in the number of hours to be worked, then simple arithmetic—multiplying the number of hours worked by the cents per hour requested—will give the total increase. However, if changes are planned, then a subdivision of workers by number of hours worked by job category, department, or other management control division will be required.

In addition, the possible impact of the increase on overtime, fringes, and other costs should be checked. Knowing the cost of each one-cent wage increase will facilitate computing changes in union requests during negotiating sessions.

Cost Per Hour

Closely aligned to the cents-per-hour figure, cost-per-hour information is generally given in cents-per-hour form. The first requirement in figuring the cost per hour of a benefit is to define the term "hour." It could be defined to mean actual hours worked by employees or by multiplying days of business operation by 8 (8-hour day x 5-day week x 52 weeks = 2,080 hours). There are other configurations of hours that are used. One is the scheduled work year, which is the number of weeks worked per year multiplied by the number of hours worked per week. Other methods include:

1) Straight-time productive hours scheduled for the work year minus any paid time off. Paid time includes vacations, holidays, and personal leave time.
2) Total productive time, which is scheduled work plus overtime.
3) Some companies try to hit a medium between scheduled work year and the smaller figure of straight-time productive hours and opt for 2,000 hours.

Note also that many requests for benefits, especially in unionized firms, are presented in a cents-per-hour cost figure (Heisel and Skinner 1976). This form is valuable for informing employees of the cost of benefits because it can easily be related to their hourly pay rate. This technique allows for flexibility and is, therefore, easy to use in bargaining situations. The total cost or impact of the figure can be found by multiplying it times the total hours worked by the employee.

Combination of Techniques to Figure a Wage Increase

Consider the familiar possibility of combining a union request for a certain desired percentage increase with a cents-per-hour minimum. The general terminology for this type of request is X percent and X number of cents per hour, whichever is greater (for example, ten percent or eighty cents per hour, whichever is greater). If the union should demand ten percent or eighty cents per hour, whichever is greater, wages for all employees in pay categories in excess of $8.00 per hour will be increased on a percentage basis, while wages for those employees in pay categories below $8.00 per hour will be increased on a cents-per-hour basis.

An obvious disadvantage to this type of demand is the compression of wage differences between skill levels. Over time, the difference in pay between skill levels tends to narrow substantially, which can lead to worker motivation problems in the higher skill categories.

COST-OF-LIVING ADJUSTMENT CLAUSE

When cost-of-living adjustment (COLA) or escalator clauses first entered into the negotiation forum, they were looked upon by some as enlightened. They provided protection for workers against pay increases over and above periodic pay adjustments, which were made according to a formula based on the Consumer Price Index (CPI). This clause increased in popularity with union members to where it is now present in 48 percent of union contracts (BNA 1983). To be more precise, in 1978 contract terms the average unit size covered by a COLA clause was 6,800 workers versus 3,000 without a COLA clause. Escalator provisions are present in 38 percent of agreements in units of 1,000 to 4,999 workers. As it now appears, the larger the bargaining unit, the greater the possibility of COLA coverage. For units of 50,000 to 99,000 workers, COLA coverage is present in 78 percent of the cases, and is present in all contracts with 100,000 workers or more (Sheifer 1979).

At the time COLA clauses first entered the negotiation forum, productivity was growing more rapidly than inflation. Recently, according to many economists, the picture has changed. Price increases and inflation have outdistanced productivity increases, which has resulted in different decisions for management negotiators.

The typical adjustment formula calls for some amount per-hour adjustment for each measured increase in the CPI. The most popular index used is the National All Cities Consumer Price Index. The COLA or escalator clause is usually combined with some form of deferred wage increase.

Frequency of adjustment to workers' hourly pay is an important issue to be negotiated. There is a compounding effect of adding the increase, especially when other wage issues such as overtime are considered. Adjustments are most often figured on a quarterly basis. Quarterly adjustments are mentioned in 60 percent of contracts with COLA clauses. This is followed by annual adjustments mentioned in 26 percent of contracts (BNA 1983). A small number of agreements are written so that COLAs are paid only when the CPI rises to an agreed-upon figure. Pay adjustments are given for increases above this level.

Cost-of-living adjustments create numerous problems in costing labor contracts. Forces creating the necessity for adjustment tend to be outside the typical areas of management control—for example, changes in the economy. To cite an instance, by the early 1980s the COLA clause accounted for 60 percent of a steelworker's total annual wage increase (Henderson 1985). Labor negotiators can help pinpoint the upper limit of labor cost exposure through establishing upper limits or "caps" for the COLA clauses. The cap on an agreement sets the maximum amount that may be added during each adjustment time period specified in the agreement.

Several cautions need to be highlighted in dealing with caps to these clauses:

1) The cap should be specified for each adjustment period. This avoids exhausting the yearly agreed-upon maximum in any one adjustment period.
2) The impact of the clause on other contract costs should be considered. Careful bargaining regarding whether the clause applies to base pay only or to various fringe benefits, overtime pay, vacation pay, pension, and insurance contributions must be done.
3) If possible, companies, especially public sector groups, should avoid signing a contract without a cap.

DIFFERENTIALS, REPORT-IN PAY, AND OVERTIME

Any discussion on wages requires some attention to various forms of supplementary pay. Paying extra for late shifts is required in 83 percent of contracts, and more than likely the absence of a premium in the contract reflects the lack of late shift work (BNA 1983). Shift differential payments generally represent a flat rate in a cents-per-hour premium for workers who must work other than normal operating times. In a minority of cases, the premium is a percentage of worker pay rates. Shift differentials tend to be larger for third shifts than for second shifts.

Employees who report for work but find none available are guaranteed "reporting pay" in 77 percent of contracts. However, in slightly over half of the cases, the guarantee is void if conditions are beyond the control of management. The amount of pay guaranteed varies from one to eight hours overall. Fifty-six percent of contracts guarantee four hours; 13 percent guarantee two hours; and 9 percent guarantee a full eight hours pay (Bureau of Labor Statistics 1980).

Similarly, to cover cases where workers are called in to work at times other than those regularly scheduled, 58 percent of contracts guarantee "call-back" or "call-in" pay. The amount of pay varies from one hour to eight hours and may have a premium attached to the pay rate (50 percent of contracts provide for a premium to be added to call-in pay). The most common guarantee is for four hours, found in 70 percent of current contracts (Bureau of Labor Statistics 1980).

Wage increases that are agreed upon will have an added impact if overtime provisions are common. This impact should be figured as part of the cost of any agreed wage increase. Perhaps the most acceptable means found to compute this cost is by using historical data to ascertain what can be expected in the way of overtime hours in the future. Data needed for costing this work should be aggregated by job classification, department, and so forth. The legal standard rate for overtime pay is 1.5 times the normal pay rate. The rate is often up to two times the normal rate in many industries. Proper costing of these data can help companies analyze alternatives, which can include adding part-time employees if these costs are excessive.

MULTIYEAR CONTRACTS

Based on survey results by the Bureau of National Affairs, *Basic Patterns in Union Contracts,* 77 percent of union contracts are for a three-year period. There are advantages to both parties to have the contract period extend for more than one year. For example, longer contract periods allow companies to compute their labor costs for an advance time period. The cost of benefits in a multiyear contract may carry considerably, based on how and when benefit changes are added to workers' pay. That is, a wage increase in effect for only six months will cost half the amount of one in effect for an entire year.

Single-year contracts now make up only 1 percent of the total as compared to 2 percent in 1979 and 5 percent in 1975. Two-year agreements account for 17 percent of labor contracts as compared to 22 percent in 1979. The longer-term agreements, those extending four or more years, make up only 4 percent (BNA 1983).

Such things as deferred wage increases are included in 94 percent of contracts, which is up since 1975. Deferred increases include annual improvement factors and productivity increases. Most (8 percent) of the increases take effect the second year of the contract, while only a small group are instituted quarterly or semiannually.

Wage-opener clauses allow for renegotiation of wages during the contract term. These clauses are those not previously discussed that relate to COLA or deferred wage increases. They are found in 7 percent of contracts (BNA 1983).

A wage increase has an obvious impact on the total cost of any demand. Options with end loads are the most expensive. The least expensive are those options that spread the increase in a more even fashion. For union negotiators, the more front-end money they can deliver to the rank-and-file the better. It becomes the management team's job to convince the union that alternative timing of wage increases will still result in satisfying the rank-and-file.

Note that while the union membership would desire a greater amount of money up front, a two-year contract without a second-year increase would not in all probability be desirable. Compensation specialists report that the effect of a raise has limited motivational life, varying from 20 days to perhaps several months. The two-year time span goes well beyond this point.

ADD-ON COST

To complete the costing picture for wages to this point, some discussion about add-on cost becomes essential. What is referred to as "add-on" cost is also referred to as "roll-up" or "creep" cost. When the one-percent and one-cent figures were arrived at earlier, the dollar amount indicated only the cost of straight-time wages. As anyone who has studied the costing problem is aware, the costs of a wage increase involve more than the actual wages themselves. For example, there are certain benefits that increase as wages increase.

While most companies recognize that an increase in direct wages will result in an increase in other benefit costs, few appear to be systematic in their approach to addressing this issue. That is, many negotiators simply add a fixed percentage to the cost of wages. Survey work by Michael Granof found that companies may not do a complete analysis of these costs and tend to use the same percentage figure year after year. Furthermore, many companies fail to recognize that basing add-on cost increases on historical or last contract figures may be misleading. If fringe benefits are to be negotiated along with direct wage increases, then historical figures may underestimate the true cost of the proposed contract request.

The only value of using current cost data to arrive at a percentage figure to compute add-on cost is to have some price estimate of the total effect of a proposed wage increase. The principal assumption to be understood when using current or historical cost figures is that future benefits will remain the same, percentagewise, as they were in the past.

If the current cost of benefit programs is to serve as an effective guide in developing wage increase agreements, individual add-on figures should be computed for each category as they are agreed upon. Computer facilities in organizations can greatly facilitate this work.

Not all benefits change with salary or wage level. Those that do not should be excluded when figuring the true one-percent or one-cent figure for negotiating purposes. They should be added back when figuring the final total cost of company benefits and in any transmittals of information showing total effective pay received by employees.

Other items often provided for workers include safety equipment, wash-up time, rest periods, lunch periods, jury duty, bereavement, and Christmas gifts. If these are included in the benefit program, their cost should be included when computing the add-on figure.

Some companies separate costs that are required by law and include old-age benefits, survivors' disability, health insurance, unemployment compensation, workmen's compensation, and certain state benefits. The separation exercise should not result in failing to add these figures to the negotiable list to derive the true one-percent and one-cent figures.

SUMMARY

This chapter is designed to lead the reader through the difficult area of costing wages and economic fringe benefits. It begins by examining the wage-productivity debate, which concerns the fact that wage increases have outpaced productivity gains in recent years. The impact of unions on wage levels is then examined. The first section also includes a look at the basic determinants of wage policy. These include area wage competition, company policy, and ability to pay.

Five areas regarding costing wages and wage-related items are discussed. These include total annual cost, cost per employee per year, percent of payroll, cents per hour, and cost per hour.

Other wage-related items such as cost of living, multiyear contracts, and add-on cost conclude the chapter. Note that while cost-of-living adjustments serve as a way to protect workers from inflation, it is an area where costs can quickly get out of hand when not carefully monitored and may require such elements as an upward adjustment limit. Consider also that multiyear contracts present special problems in negotiations. Changes in pay and benefits can substantially influence the total cost of a collective bargaining agreement.

Add-on costs are also discussed. These are the summation of benefit items that can equal 30 to 50 percent of straight-time payroll cost. If not included in figuring the total payroll package, large errors can result.

9   Costing Benefits

INTRODUCTION

Benefit packages in many companies exceed 30 percent of the total payroll cost (Henderson 1985) and must also be costed accurately. In a 1982 survey by the U.S. Chamber of Commerce, employee benefits averaged 36.7 percent of payroll costs:

Employer-required payments	— 9.5 percent
Employer share of pension, insurance, and other agreed-to payments	—13.1 percent
Paid rest periods, lunch periods	— 2.8 percent
Vacations, sick leave, holidays	— 9.1 percent
Profit-sharing and bonus payments	— 2.2 percent
Total	—36.7 percent

The per-employee benefit figure across all industries equaled $3.52 per hour and $7,187 per year.

Percentages have increased at a dramatic rate over time. For instance, the 1929 figure is 3 percent; in 1959 it increased to 19 percent; and in 1969 the package of fringe benefits as a percent of the total payroll cost grew to 24 percent. Gross dollar amounts have increased from $1,268 per employee to $6,837 per employee per year from 1959 to 1979 according to longitudinal tracking of 182 companies by the U.S. Chamber of Commerce. This amounts to a 439 percent increase.

The increase in total benefits can be tied in part to the higher cost of individual benefits. In addition, new benefits have been added, including those required by federal, state, and local statutes. Another factor impacting on the increase in benefits is the role benefit packages can have in improving employee perceptions of well-being and, therefore, in improving productivity for the company.

Research in the field suggests, however, that companies may not be getting the return they expect on this form of investment. One reason may be that employees often place minimal value on these benefits, take them for granted, or do not consider them as incentives for increased productivity (Henderson 1985). This may be due to a failure to communicate the value of the benefits to employees in a detailed and clear manner. This, in turn, may be due to the fact that many companies have not performed a sufficient cost analysis of the benefit packages and, therefore, do not have accurate figures to convey to employees (Henderson 1985). Knowing the cost of a benefit package is essential before communication with employees can take place, not to mention its importance in determining the long-range impact of benefit costs on company operations and making appropriate management decisions in labor contract negotiations.

Union negotiators must also assume responsibility for costing demands in this area. Full analysis by the union team guards against irresponsible demands and arms it with reliable data to use in arguing a given position.

Fringe benefits and certain noneconomic benefits may constitute nonproductive time payments. There is no doubt that vacations, holidays, and other benefits are reasonable, or that a longer break may increase employee productivity. The focus of attention should be on how to cost these items, the assumption being that, unless research shows otherwise, benefits do indeed have a positive effect on employee productivity.

Most labor contracts have noneconomic clauses or clauses that address matters that appear to be incidental in nature. These clauses are perceived as having less financial impact than economic clauses, are primarily of a policy-setting nature, and address issues from the local union setting.

Frequently, these clauses result in important financial considerations. The perceived proportion of a new cost adjustment to overall labor costs is often not great. As a result, the item is dismissed as immaterial. A 1985 U.S. Chamber of Commerce survey indicated that these benefits can account for approximately 4 percent of total payroll costs.

Consider, for example, the impact of contract provisions relating to "work assignments." This area is considered noneconomic by most companies. But if changes occur that permit workers to have their own choice of job assignments using seniority as a basis, then management flexibility is limited. The company cannot assign the most qualified person to the job, and efficiency declines. Granof's findings showed that few companies attempt to take such points into account during negotiations. A job-bid system clause negotiated into a 1968 coal industry contract altered management prerogative in job assignments, which has had an impact on productivity. The exact extent to which productivity is affected has not been measured; however, coal industry managers are aware that the job-bid clause is not a noneconomic item (Holoviak 1980).

This chapter will discuss costing of economic and noneconomic fringe benefits, beginning with the economic fringe benefits and ending with the noneconomic fringe benefits.

ECONOMIC FRINGE BENEFITS

Costing Holiday Pay

It is common for companies to offer employees from nine to twelve paid holidays per year. The median number is ten, which is up from nine in prior years (Henderson 1985 and Bureau of Labor Statistics 1980). Prior to the recession in 1982, there was a trend toward increasing the number of paid holidays. Various labor agreements signed during the recession, which was a period of reverse collective bargaining, actually reduced the number of holidays. It is difficult to judge if the future trend will be toward increasing or decreasing the number of employee holidays. In addition, some companies offer from one to three floating holidays, to be chosen by the employee or by mutual agreement with the employer.

The most commonly offered holidays include the following:

New Year's Day	Labor Day
Good Friday	Thanksgiving Day
Memorial Day	Christmas Day
Independence Day	

Other commonly offered holidays include the following:

Washington's Birthday	Friday after
Columbus Day	Thanksgiving
Presidential Election Day	Christmas Eve
Veterans' Day	New Year's Eve

Employees can work on the holiday for extra pay. It is generally recommended that employee eligibility for holiday or premium pay for working a holiday be contingent upon the employee working the days before and after. The rationale when the employee is taking the holiday is to reduce the possibility of a holiday's extending into a minivacation, which can create numerous staffing problems. The rationale when the employee is working the holiday is to preclude the employee's taking a day off, working the holiday, and earning two day's pay.

In addition, when the regulars are not working, it may be necessary to recruit replacement workers. The cost of these workers must be included in the cost of the benefit. Again, accurate records regarding the historical impact of holidays and any overtime or replacement help needed can be used as predicators of future cost.

According to Michael Granof (1973), there are other expenses involved with holiday pay (as there are with sick pay and paid vacations) that are frequently overlooked. For the most part, computing the cost of hiring temporary help includes only the wage paid multiplied by the number of hours worked. Yet there are other costs that are often overlooked, including:

advertising	company badges and safety equipment
references	indoctrination and training
employment agencies	security and credit investigation
break-in time	severance pay
letter of application	extra Social Security taxes
application blanks	insurance costs
interview by personnel	increased unemployment

Costing Paid Vacations

A key benefit in the area of pay for nonproductive time is the granting of annual vacations to employees. Any method of computing the cost for this benefit depends on the manner of compensating the employee. Those who receive a regular salary will receive this as their vacation benefit (Henderson 1985). However, those who are paid on an incentive basis may receive only what would be their "draw" amount, or have their pay based on some average earnings for some time frame before the vacation.

Eligibility for vacation is normally based on tenure periods of employees: one week vacation after six months of service, two weeks for one to three years of service, and so forth. To calculate the cost of this benefit, it becomes necessary to keep accurate records of the employee work force in terms of length of service on the job and pay schedule. In addition, it is necessary to have knowledge regarding how vacation periods are determined and the length of benefit for each employee.

To determine the true cost of this benefit, it is necessary to know whether vacationing employees will be replaced with temporary employees. This implies the cost per hour of the replacement, which involves the base rate of pay; the prorated cost of recruiting, testing, and so forth; plus any fringe benefits for temporary workers, such as Social Security, workmen's compensation, and a group of benefits not required by law but agreed to by management. To determine the long-run cost implications of these benefits, certain questions must be answered: Can an employee accumulate benefits over a period of years and receive the benefit upon retirement? Can the employee receive extra pay by working instead of taking the vacation? Do part-time and nonexempt workers qualify for vacation benefits? In retailing, for example, most firms do grant vacations to all employees (Gable and Hollon 1977).

Vacation clauses for workers appear in 91 percent of all contracts. Most recent BNA surveys reveal the trend toward five- and six-week vacations and reduced requirements for service time to the company to qualify. One-week vacations are less frequent than two-, or three-, or four-week vacations, due to more contracts providing for a minimum of two weeks for all employees, regardless of tenure. Eighty-three percent of contracts state the basis for computing vacation pay. Slightly more than half of contracts pay at base rate of pay and one-third pay on employee average earnings (BNA 1983; Major Collective Agreements 1980).

Compression, which refers to the process of reducing tenure requirements for eligibility for benefits, is an increasingly important point for negotiators to consider. It has a definite effect on the cost per hour of the vacation benefit. It is also useful to understand the cost of additional weeks of vacation, as it is not unusual during normal economic conditions for additional vacation weeks to be requested in negotiation situations.

Costing Pensions and Profit Sharing

Pensions and profit sharing are areas for which the advice and counsel of specialists are not just helpful, but mandatory. Early pension and profit-sharing payments were not nearly so complicated as they are now. Currently, they must provide decent retirement benefits and simultaneously satisfy numerous requirements of both federal and state agencies and laws. Pension plans are incorporated into 90 percent of contracts and, along with Social Security cost, account for some 35 percent of the total cost of all benefits offered by a company (Henderson 1985 and Granof 1973).

For pension cost to be a legitimate deductible business expense on employer taxes, it must qualify according to various Internal Revenue Codes. In addition, the Employee Retirement Income Security Act of 1974 (ERISA) mandates that many tough provisions be included in pension plans. If the company is unionized, then the employer must also permit its union to have a voice in the plan's administration.

Currently, according to Belcher (1974), most plans fall into a few forms. These are group pensions, deferred or cash profit sharing, and savings plans:

1) Group pensions are the basic model, and are frequently combined with profit-sharing and savings plans. Normally included is mandatory coverage of all employees and is either paid in total by company or some form of cost sharing with the employees.

2) Profit-sharing plans, deferred or cash, normally involve setting aside certain amounts of company profit for each employee. Upon the retirement, death, or other agreed-upon circumstances, the benefits are distributed to the employee or their chosen beneficiaries. Tax advantages and accrued interest make these plans attractive to employees. The ultimate test of their usefulness as an incentive depends in large measure on the vesting provisions. Vesting time is the amount of time an employee must be working before having full rights to the funds. A very famous example of deferred distribution is the Sears & Roebuck plan that has worked very well to provide satisfactory retirement benefits and has also worked effectively as an employee incentive.

Cash or current profit-sharing plans (not as popular as deferred plans) represent about 40 percent of total profit-sharing arrangements. Normally found in smaller organizations, the funds are paid out as soon as possible after profits are earned. Usually the distribution is made monthly or quarterly. It has been estimated that 75,000 cash plans were in effect in 1971 versus over 100,000 deferred plans.

3) Savings plans are used to stimulate employee savings for retirement. The incentive provided by the company is in some form of matching funds, which range from 50 to 100 percent of employee contributions to the plan. These plans have a stated limit, which is usually in a range of 5 to 10 percent of the employee base pay. The funds are then placed in one of various types of investment arrangements.

Generally, the cost of any proposed changes in pension plans are given to consulting or staff actuaries. Companies provide the necessary demographic data and the cost of the plan is based on the traditional techniques used by actuary companies and quoted in terms of total annual cost or a cents-per-hour figure. What the company outlay will be depends on the actuarial cost-method used. The "entry-age normal method," which assumes a standard entry age, is the most widely used technique. Benefits are usually amortized over 30 years (Granof 1973).

Companies must always be careful in adjusting benefits without a thorough examination of all ramifications. Two examples offered by Heisel and Skinner (1976) reinforce this fact. First, if a company decides to help persons already retired by changing the plan to allow for postretirement adjustment to reflect Consumer Price Index (CPI) increases, it may be difficult to project accurate costs. This sort of change makes it hard for consulting actuaries to give the company accurate figures as to what pension costs will be in the future. Second, any automatic wage adjustment added to help current employees keep pace with changes in economic conditions will make it very difficult to predict wage levels at retirement. The wage-level prediction at retirement is the key point of information in determining both future benefits and company contribution level to provide such benefits.

In addition to the above, Heisel and Skinner (1976) suggest various other questions that should be considered when costing pension benefits:

1) Will the employee share in pension cost? Will his contribution be funded immediately and be "portable" to go with the employee when leaving the company?
2) What is the relationship of benefits to length of service? Are there any provisions for early retirement?
3) When will the employee have full right to the contribution of the employer? (Certain legislation requires private plans to provide vesting according to various formulas.)

Actuaries tend not to offer opinions on the efficacy of company policy. Their input is of a technical nature: they figure the cost of company plans and plan changes. The company must decide, for example, whether it will provide continuing benefits during periods when senior employees are laid off. Company policy also tends to dictate the minimum plan benefits, that is, how retirement benefits will be paid.

Age 65 is specified as normal retirement age in 91 percent of the plans. The range varies from 55 to 70 years. Minimum service requirement is specified in 58 percent of contracts. These range from five to 25 years, with 66 percent requiring ten years of service, and only 7 percent requiring 25 years of service (BNA 1983).

Costing Life Insurance

Life insurance protection for employees is provided by almost every company. The BNA study showed that life insurance is present in 98 percent of manufacturing and 93 percent of nonmanufacturing contracts analyzed. The cost of coverage is paid by the company in most cases. The BNA study showed that 87 percent of benefit plans were paid for by the company, while the cost is shared in 13 percent of the cases (BNA 1983).

Many types and varieties of insurance plans are available, including group life, health and hospitalization, dental and vision, disability, legal, liability,and supplemental unemployment benefit (SUB) insurance. Regardless of type or kind, actuaries are needed to make precise judgments regarding the financial impact of these plans. Several different approaches may be used. The company can set aside money each year to meet anticipated claims under a "self-insurance" plan. This approach should be used only with large numbers of employees and large corporate entities. The process can be risky and is most often found in public institutions (Henderson 1985). Commercial insurers can also be used. This is most often done through a bidding process or by individual contract arrangement in conjunction with skilled actuaries. Company-sponsored life insurance programs, which offer a modicum of financial stability for the family in the event of the death of the employee, can also be used.

For the most part, life insurance plans are offered as part of a group plan, which is able to offer the benefit of lower rates due to the fact that all employees are enrolled. The general guide businesses should follow is for the benefit to equal two years of the employee's total wages or salary.

Options to be considered include offering increased benefit dollars as the worker's tenure with the company increases and offering workers the opportunity to purchase added amounts at nominal fees and to purchase coverage for family dependents (Henderson 1985). Coverage payment normally results in companies paying 100 percent of the premiums and workers paying for options. Other less frequent contribution splits range from 80 percent employer, 20 percent worker to 50-50 for each party.

According to Henderson (1985), standard life insurance features include total worker participation, with the health status of the individual not taken into account. Conversion to an individual policy can be arranged if the worker decided to discontinue employment. This usually must take place within 30 days or some other specified time. Worker coverage may also be continued for 30 days upon leaving the company or upon retirement.

Bargaining over insurance benefits generally takes one of two courses. Either a defined set of benefits might be demanded by the union or a certain amount of money is to be allocated for certain benefits. In the case of a defined set of benefits, the management negotiator needs accurate long-term bids from insurance companies. Asking only one carrier could result in an inflated price as it cannot be assumed all insurance companies offer the same prices. In cases where a certain amount of money is to be allocated for certain benefits, caution must be used not to buy what appears to be the biggest bag of benefits for the fixed dollar amount without thorough investigation. Benefits that are too small will result in poor employee relations now and demands for large increases in later contracts.

Costing Health Insurance

Hospitalization expense coverage is seen in 85 percent of labor contracts. Of this group, 31 percent use plans like Blue Cross, 26 percent use private commercial carriers, 9 percent use health maintenance coverage, and 19 percent use other plans. Total cost of expenses is provided for in 81 percent of plans and 79 percent pay duration of illness for hospitalization benefits (BNA 1983).

Dependents are covered in 91 percent of plans, up from 75 percent in 1979. The coverage is equal in value to that of the employees. Ninety percent of plans provide for the employer to pay the full cost and the other 10 percent have both sharing the costs. Surgical coverage is as common as hospitalization coverage. Similarly, major medical is almost as common, specified in 74 percent of contracts (BNA 1983).

Health insurance benefits cover virtually all employees in the majority of companies, with most including major medical provisions as part of the package. The plans contain a limitless variety of assistance-type programs. A recent survey across industry groups reveals that dental plans are included in 41 percent of the contracts and 30 percent have prescription drug programs ("Compensation Currents . . ." 1979). The above survey shows that the cost of this service has increased over recent years. Its findings are supported by the survey work of Michael Granof (1973), who found the cost of accident and health insurance becoming a larger portion of labor cost. For example, in a recent *Wall Street Journal* article, it was reported that General Motors spent $3,270 on health benefits for each of its 522,000 employees in 1981. This figure reflects a 12 percent increase from 1980 and a 113 percent increase from the 1975 figure of $1,534 per employee. According to Henderson (1985), basic types of medical plans in the hospital and surgical area include:

1) Hospitalization plans offered by commercial insurance companies provide fixed cash benefits for hospital room and board plus other stated hospital costs. These plans can pay directly to the hospital or to the insured, who in turn pays the hospital. Blue Cross service plans systems are slightly different from commercial plans. They pay the hospital directly for room, board, and necessary hospital services in lieu of direct cash payments to the individual.

2) Expanded plans include diagnostic visits to the medical doctor's office and an annual physical.

3) Vision care and dental care benefits are important and popular additions to medical coverage to protect workers from the cost of these needed services.

One factor that should be remembered in any computation of costs of health insurance is the total effect or the "spillover" effect. Health insurance is provided to all employees, union and nonunion, as are most benefits. It is important to note that any benefit changes granted to the covered workers will also be given to those not covered by the collective bargaining agreement. When figuring the cost of the agreement, be sure to compute any spillover effects for nonunion workers.

Costing Sick Pay

Most companies report a policy that allows employees to take time off for being sick without loss of job or pay. Most of these benefits are funded by the company up to a point, after which commercial insurance plans will often pick up the tab for extended absences.

Cost estimates for a sick leave plan are based on accurate recordkeeping of the number of days sick by the various classifications of workers. A historical trend line is the best estimate possible for future demands, barring any new source of data for more accurate predictions. How generous the plan and whether or not there is any allowance for personal business leave will help figure the degree of usage. The accumulation of sick leave is a policy matter. Some companies allow sick leave to accumulate and be taken at retirement, although many companies put limits on the maximum number of days (100 is common) that can be carried at any given time.

Another factor that must be remembered is replacement cost for sick workers if such action is necessary for continued operation. Of course, any contemplated wage increases will increase the cost of this benefit. Paid sick leave is provided in 28 percent of contracts with 92 percent of these provisions calling for the regular pay rate (BNA 1983).

Cafeteria-Type Benefit Selection

A rather new approach being used in some organizations is to allow employees to choose the benefits they wish to receive on an individual basis. From the cost analysis vantage point, these open-choice situations enable the company to explain the cost and worth of individual benefit programs to employees. In theory, the employees have a pool of funds to spend on benefits, know the cost of each item purchased, and know how much money remains in the pool for added selection. The pool for that person is exhausted when benefit purchases use up the allotted funds.

Note, however, that some benefits (such as Social Security) are mandated by law. Benefits mandated by law and by contractual agreement with the union will reduce the pool of available funds for individual selection of benefits.

These flexible plans, often referred to as "cafeteria" plans, are said to accomplish four basic goals in a sound compensation program. They display a desire on the part of the employer to improve the employee's quality of life, enhance employee output, heighten employee awareness of the values and costs of benefits supplied by the organization, and add to employee understanding of the value and cost of total benefit programs (Henderson 1985).

Allowing individual choice can result in the organization's incurring higher costs. With all employees participating in each category, the cost of a benefit can be reduced. With reduced numbers participating by selecting other benefits, the cost may increase for some benefits.

There is no strong evidence to suggest that cafeteria plans are overwhelming successes. Because of high numbers of mandated and agreed-upon benefits, choice is reduced significantly. In these cases, the flexibility that allows the selection of benefits important to young workers (such as maternity) and older workers (pension) may be so slight as to be meaningless. Yet, selection options are on the increase. For example, 23 percent of hospitalization provisions in union contracts allow employees to choose between different types of coverage (BNA 1983).

Costing of benefits under a cafeteria-type flexible plan is the same as costing of benefits under any other plans. The main difference comes in the data collection and storage by the organization, where it may require more time and effort to track the individual differences.

Statutory Benefits

Obvious by their absence from the above are statutory insurance and other benefit coverage. Among the programs of this type are Social Security (old age, survivors', and disability insurance), workmen's compensation, unemployment, and disability insurance.

Because of the precise requirements set forth in those areas, most companies are aware of these costs. However, to be complete in costing the benefit package, these must be added because of their large cost. These costs now average 9 percent of the payroll cost. The requirements for some of these benefits vary from state to state, and the Social Security costs are ever increasing.

Total Cost of Negotiated Benefits

Benefit costs accumulate quickly. The individual costs for some appear slight, only one cent or three cents per hour. Collectively, they can increase to between 30 and 40 percent of straight-time pay.

Not every possible economic benefit has been discussed. The principal ones were covered. Benefits classified as economic by some may be classified as noneconomic by others. Jury duty, wash-up time, uniforms, company business, and paid lunch are some controversial benefits that will be discussed in the next section. In actual costing situations one will find that consideration of the costs of benefits can double (or more than double) the increase in costs for items being negotiated. They are well worth costing accurately.

NONECONOMIC FRINGE BENEFITS

Paid Lunch, Rest Periods, and Wash-Up Time

Paid lunch, rest periods, and wash-up time are considered to be noneconomic benefits. Table 4.1 indicates the frequency of occurrence of each benefit in manufacturing and nonmanufacturing contracts.

A Bureau of National Affairs survey (1979) indicated that for agreements that specify the amount of lunch time granted, 66 percent are for 30 minutes and 23 percent are for 60 minutes. However, in 17 percent of contracts, if an employee works through the scheduled lunch period, overtime pay provisions are provided.

Rest periods are approached from two perspectives. In 10 percent of the cases they are governed by past practice in the plant. In most cases they are governed by detailed contract provisions that specify when, how long, and how many rest periods are agreed to by the parties. The majority of contracts offer two rest periods per shift, with 50 percent allowing ten minutes and 40 percent allowing 15 minutes (BNA 1983).

Wash-up or clean-up time is mentioned in 22 percent of the contracts (BNA 1983). However, the terms used are general and can mean either actual personal cleaning or changing of clothes. The time specified is either five or ten minutes, with five being the more frequent.

TABLE 9.1. Frequency of Noneconomic Benefits

Benefit	Percent Across all Contracts	Percent Manufacturing	Percent Nonmanufacturing
Paid lunch	48	43	56
Rest periods	34	32	36
Wash-up time	20	22	16

Source: Compiled from Bureau of National Affairs (BNA), Basic Patterns in Union Contracts (Washington, D.C.: Bureau of National Affairs, 1979), 30–32.

The cost of these contract provisions is simply the cost in dollars divided by the hours worked. When paid lunch, rest periods, and wash-up time are considered together, the cost is substantial.

Some additional comments are necessary to complete the discussion regarding these items. All three benefits will be provided for both employees covered by the union contract and those not covered, such as secretaries, staff workers, and non-exempt workers, thereby increasing the true cost of these items. This is referred to as the spillover effect and is covered in more detail in a later section.

In addition, there are instances in which it might be necessary to use overtime pay rates rather than straight-time pay rates. The assumption made when using straight-time pay rates is that workers' production capability is increased due to the above allowances for time away from the job; therefore, their production rate is not affected—they continue to produce 100 widgets a day. However, this is not true, and the production rate is lower. In these instances, overtime hours may be needed to make up that lost production. These costs must be included in overall cost calculations.

Paid Leave for Jury Duty

Figuring the cost of paid leave for jury duty is difficult. Precise figures are not readily available. The best technique is the use of the historical trendline: analysis of what it has cost in past years and the projection of these costs into the future. The cost per hour figure is computed by dividing the total dollar cost to the company by the number of hours worked.

Leave to perform jury duty or other forms of court or civil responsibility is provided for in 83 percent of contracts. Payment is the employee's regular wage less any fee received. Thirteen percent of the contracts in the BNA sample did place limits on the number of paid jury leave days (BNA 1983).

Bereavement Pay

Paid leave for a death in the family is difficult to project in precise dollar terms. The best alternative is to use some form of historical index to estimate future costs. The number of contracts offering this benefit increased from 57 percent in 1971 to 80 percent in 1979 and to 82 percent in 1983. Of the contracts granting funeral leave, 90 percent give three days, with the remaining 10 percent offering between one and five days (BNA 1983).

Meetings Between Management and Union Leaders

Meetings between management and union leaders have become a popular mechanism for promoting effective communication between these groups. This area of interaction draws heavily from Japanese management models, particularly their quality circles. For example, 45 percent of labor contracts now call for safety-health committees, and union-management cooperative clauses are included in 37 percent of contracts, up from 12 percent in 1975 (BNA 1983).

A program proposal to improve the quality of communication between management and labor has many farsighted benefits. On the other hand, these forums can be just ego trips for union and management leaders. Such programs will require committee members to be excused from their jobs to attend meetings, incurring costs for lost production time and possible travel expenses. In such cases, the demand should be viewed carefully.

Various forms of committees are becoming popular and cost-benefit analysis should be instituted early to ensure they are productive. Remember, some committee members may be performing critical jobs and may need to be replaced during the time spent in meetings.

Cost-benefit analysis should include a wide category of items to judge the effectiveness of the program. Some of the points to monitor include: changes on scrap or waste, reject rate, absenteeism, tardiness, customer returns, illness rates, output (productivity), changes in cost basis, and grievance rates.

Labor contract analysts need to monitor all elements in the cost benefit list, since it is common to see initial productivity decline when joint-effort committees are utilized. Unfortunately, currently most of these efforts will be done more for show by both sides than out of any genuine attempt to jointly increase productivity. It is particularly important to gather accurate costing data at contract expiration to substantiate party positions for the renewal contract.

Union Business

Leave from work assignments to perform union duties exists in 85 percent of manufacturing contracts (BNA 1979).

However, research by Granof found that few companies take the time to cost such proposals. Categories of union business typically include situations where a union office is representing an employee to management and those areas that are strictly union business. Table 9.2 data show the result of a Bureau of Labor Statistics survey reflecting types of business for which union members are paid and the number of agreements that offer pay for each type of activity.

Customarily, stewards and officers process grievances on company time. In only 15 percent of all contracts is the number of hours paid to stewards for handling grievances limited. In just 22 percent of clauses, the time is limited by vague terms, such as "unreasonable or excessive" (Bureau of Labor Statistics 1980, Henderson 1985).

Those firms that did evaluate the cost of contract changes involving union business computed it by taking the number of hours paid to stewards times their wage rates. Other cost estimates must be added to arrive at a complete cost that will reflect leave for strictly union business plus the above. These include:

1) cost of witness to testify at a grievance hearing;
2) cost of salary for full-time union officers;
3) cost of benefits for full-time union officers;
4) cost of replacement for full-time union officers; and
5) any possible estimate for lost productivity (Granof 1973).

It is difficult for anyone to cost a union request worded in such vague terms as "reasonable" time and an "appropriate" or "sufficient" number of stewards to conduct business. Means by which this cost can be controlled include limiting the number of stewards through a contract clause or limiting the number of hours per a given time frame that can be used for steward business. Clarification of these two points in the contract can aid in determining cost. In addition, past records regarding how many grievances were filed and how many conventions and other activities union delegates and officers attended will provide useful information.

It is not unusual for unions to request clauses in the contract providing for fully paid leave to attend both state and international union conventions. If five officers and delegates are excused for this strictly union business, 50 working days are lost for two one-week conventions. When premium pay must be granted to replace employees for 50 working days, the

TABLE 9.2. Paid Time for Union Business

Activity	Number of Agreements Paying for Activity
All agreements*	1,550
Total referring to pay for time on union business	877
Grievance and/or arbitration	317
Contract negotiations	9
Other union business**	238
Grievance, arbitration, and contract negotiations	51
Grievance, arbitration and other union business	171
Contract negotiations and other union business	8
Grievance, arbitration, negotiations, and other union business	36
Other***	47
No reference to pay for time on union business	673

*Includes agreements covering 1,000 workers or more, January 2, 1980.

**Other union business includes time spent collecting union dues, checking union cards, attending union conventions or training, attending labor-management committee meetings, and similar activities.

***Includes agreements that refer to no specific type of activity, that are unclear, or are subject to local negotiations.

Source: Bureau of Labor Statistics, Bulletin 2095 (U.S. Department of Labor, Washington, D.C., 1980), p. 95.

cost is not as immaterial as it is often perceived to be. Having these costs itemized and then computed as a cost-per-hour benefit applied to the contract package may prove to be a wise contract-costing strategy.

Working Conditions

At the beginning of this chapter, there was some discussion as to how changes in working conditions may affect productivity and profits. Another example cited from *Costing Union Demands* (Heisel and Skinner 1976) may also serve to demonstrate this area of benefit costing.

In a large public sector agency the union bargained for vacation schedules that permitted members to be granted summer vaca-cations. Not an unusual request; however, the agency's peak work load activity was also in the summer.

This clause made the employment of seasonal help as vacation replacements required. Now, instead of absorbing vacation cost during off-peak times or in lost productivity, it had to bear the expenses of added outlays for replacement workers. The cost of this clause to the agency included:
1) salaries of temporary seasonal help;
2) benefits available to them;
3) any wage differentials paid to persons temporarily promoted;
4) cost of employment processing;
5) training cost of temporary and promoted replacements; and
6) impact on productivity by having regular, more competent workers perform the job.

Employee Uniforms

There is some debate as to the negotiability of uniform requirements or work clothes required for the job. Although there appears to be no specific National Labor Relations Board (NLRB) ruling that settles the issue, work clothes are considered to be different from safety clothes and equipment.

In 32 percent of labor contracts (up from 23 percent in 1979), this item can be found across all industry classifications, making an examination of specific industry patterns helpful. Provisions for work clothes or employee uniforms are found in 89 percent of retail contracts, 72 percent of services contracts, 72 percent of transportation contracts, 69 percent of chemical contracts, 38 percent of food contracts, and 48 percent of construction contracts. Contracts that discuss uniforms require that they be supplied by the employer in 74 percent of the cases. In 51 percent of the cases, the employer is responsible for cleaning and replacing the uniforms (BNA 1983).

There is an obvious economic impact to management of providing such a benefit on a unilateral basis. In addition, the union may insist on negotiating type and quality of uniforms with a higher impact on contract cost than expected. A logical next step in negotiations would be for union leaders to request uniform maintenance subsidies, which could be quite costly.

Historical references can provide accurate primary cost data to compute this benefit in most situations. As with other benefits, this should be reduced to a cost-per-hour figure both to show employees and to enlighten management regarding the true cost of a labor agreement.

Travel Expense Reimbursement

In 28 percent of contracts (up from 19 percent in 1979) travel necessitated by the job calls for expense reimbursement (BNA 1983). In the public sector, many agencies require employees to drive their own cars on public business. Their unions will negotiate a fixed mileage rate to compensate the employee.

According to the 1983 BNA survey, reimbursement for expenses away from headquarters are allowed for in 63 percent of contracts in the construction, transportation, and utility industries. Forty-one percent of contracts in the communications, retail and utility industries allow for reimbursement for use of a personal car on company business. Thirty-five percent of contracts in the construction industry allow a daily allowance for travel; while 30 percent of contract travel clauses in the petroleum, printing, and transportation equipment industries allow reimbursement for moving and transfer expenses.

Heisel and Skinner (1976) note several good techniques for computation of the cost-of-travel reimbursement and suggestions for keeping track of those costs. Past records can be used to determine mileage paid and can be adjusted if the increases are granted. Often these data are not kept in a central file, but a minor adjustment with accounting procedures can correct this. Possibilities for requiring alternate forms of transportation such as public transit or a car from a motor pool, should be examined. A check should be made to see if any planned changes will require more travel than in the past. If so, this should be taken into consideration before going to the bargaining table.

Unemployment Benefit Programs

Supplemental Unemployment Benefit Plans

Although income security plans date back to the early 1920s, they were seldom negotiated at the bargaining table until the mid-1950s. Supplemental Unemployment Benefits (SUB) plans are designed to provide workers with financial protection against job layoff.

The company pays an agreed-upon amount (such as 7 cents per hour worked) into a SUB fund for each paid labor hour. The funds are used to supplement unemployment compensation for laid-off workers. The employee's contribution to the fund is limited. These limits are negotiated and are often stated as an overall dollar value for the fund. Supplemental unemployment benefits are divided into pooled and individual account plans. Pooled fund methods provide for pay only in the event of lack of work and are the most common plans. Individual account plans provide workers vested rights to the account and may be withdrawn in full at termination. Due to the infrequency of individual accounts, discussion will center around pooled funds.

Most plans pay a percentage of the employees' straight-pay rate, which is added to the employees' unemployment compensation. This can equal 95 percent of take-home pay. Other plans vary from 60 to 85 percent of compensation. Note that certain groups (such as Ladies' Garment Workers) pay a set lump-sum benefit per week.

Employer's liability is limited to the amount in the fund. When the fund is exhausted, no further liability exists. Therefore, forecasting costs in this area becomes a simple matter of projection of the agreed-to per-hour contribution up to the fund's limit.

Again, in this area, breaking down the cost into a per-hour figure may be helpful at negotiation time. Few companies bother even to include this item when reporting benefits to workers.

There is a possibility that management could use these for collateral for loans or to satisfy bank deposit requirements. This reduces the opportunity cost to the employer for a possibly large pool of money. Of course, details regarding the use of these funds must be agreed to in the labor contract.

Government Unemployment Programs

In most areas of the country, both private and public sector employees are covered by unemployment insurance. Between state and federal programs, some employees have received benefits for as long as 65 weeks (Henderson 1985). The goal of most companies is to reduce their required contribution to the state unemployment compensation fund through stable work scheduling. The employer is required to pay both federal and state premiums or employer insurance tax. For state levels, the amount varies with each state.

Severance Pay

Another employment security program is severance pay. Severance pay plans are present in 45 percent of manufacturing and 28 percent of nonmanufacturing contracts (BNA 1983). Many of the severance pay plans are tied into SUB plan provisions. After a stated length of time on layoff with no prospect for recall, a company may elect to issue severance pay to a worker. SUB plan benefits would then cease. A minority (15 percent) of the plans also provides severance for workers who are ineligible for pension plans.

The benefit amount is normally tied into a ratio of employee length of service. The amount ranges from one to 52 weeks. One week's pay for each year of service is the most frequently used ratio. The next most frequent is one-half week's pay for each year of service. Only 8 percent in the BNA survey of contracts paid a flat weekly amount for each year of service. Generally, a service requirement is stipulated for eligibility.

Nine percent of contracts require six months of service to be eligible for severance pay. Ten percent require five years of service, 13 percent require two, 15 percent require three, and 50 percent require only one year of service (BNA 1983).

Costing the severance pay benefit in the absence of any supporting data is usually done by investigating historical trends or assuming that last year's record will be similar to next year's. Information regarding certain economic and production forecasts should also be used in computing these costs. These could offer more insight into areas where terminations will take place.

Cafeteria Benefit

Employee dining facilities and benefits range from benches and vending machines to elaborate dining facilities. Often this service is a nonprofit operation, and food may even be offered at below-cost prices with the company absorbing the losses.

Costing this benefit follows the traditional pattern. Attention should be made to include in the cost of total payments to concessionaries all fees paid, wages for people who work in dining facilities, cost of equipment, and any direct loss on food the company absorbs.

Other Benefits and Services

There is an increasing array of benefits and services that union and management negotiators have agreed to in recent years. The obvious goal from the management perspective is enhanced employee welfare and a stronger commitment to the goals of the organization. For the union negotiators, the services are valued by their members and offer the advantage of being easier to secure in recent years than larger wage increases.

As indicated earlier, there is little evidence to suggest that companies are taking the necessary effort to compute the cost of these benefits as part of the total contract package. Many benefits are considered noneconomic in nature and may be difficult to arrive at in dollar value. However, the effort is necessary if the true total cost picture of a contract is to be determined.

According to Henderson (1985), benefits and services under this category can include:

1) Thrift or short-term savings plans.
2) Social and recreational activities.
3) Length of service awards and seniority awards.
4) Merchandise-purchasing plans.
5) Umbrella liability coverage.
6) Transportation and parking.
7) Purchase of used equipment.
8) Charter flights and tours.
9) Educational opportunities and subsidies.
10) Moving and/or transfer allowances.
11) Counseling.
12) Stock purchase plans.
13) Legal services.
14) Emergency loans.
15) Auto insurance.
16) Referral awards.
17) Gift matching.
18) Christmas bonuses.
19) Credit unions.
20) Child adoption.
21) Child care.

Techniques used to cost this group of benefits are similar to those suggested for costing cafeteria food benefits. An effort should be made to include all aspects of company cost or losses absorbed.

SUMMARY

This chapter approaches the topic of costing economic and noneconomic benefits for employees. The introduction also examines how expensive economic fringe benefits have become to business. According to various surveys, costs range from $5,560 to $6,837 per employee per year. Costs have increased for many reasons, including tax advantages to both employee and company, lack of awareness by managers as to the extent of benefits (including nonproductive time payments such as holidays and breaks).

Issues of costing the more commonly offered economic fringe benefits are also presented, including how to control the cost of certain benefit areas. The discussion also includes special efforts to alert the reader to often hidden costs of offering certain benefits. Hidden costs include such items as personnel processing time, benefits for replacement workers, training, and so forth.

In addition to voluntary benefit items, the chapter concludes with a discussion of the cost of mandatory benefits such as unemployment insurance, Social Security, and other government-required coverage.

This chapter also presents an array of items that are frequently looked upon as noneconomic in nature and discusses how to cost them. Noneconomic benefits seldom receive the attention that more traditional items receive, primarily because they are seen as representing a very small cost. Taken separately, they are inexpensive when compared to individual economic items, but when considered as a whole they can add up to a substantial cost. Problems with noneconomic benefits go beyond just the small expense of each separate item and the resultant lack of management attention.

10 Writing Agreements

INTRODUCTION

In the late 1930s, the written agreement became the basic building block of the collective bargaining process (Prasow and Peters 1983). As the legal framework changed, National Labor Relations Board rulings established certain precedents and the case history of arbitration rulings began to offer direction toward the standardization of labor contracts. In the current environment one can go to any reasonably well-supplied university library and find standard contract clauses available for guidance.

Certainly, with half a century of progress, experimentation, and learning, contracts should be rather straightforward documents. Writing should be plain and clear, offer but one distinct interpretation to clause meanings, and have only minor problems with ambiguities. Unfortunately, this is not usually the case. Some progress has taken place. Standardization has occurred, such that an experienced labor relations representative can find certain clauses with relative ease. However, as the arbitration case books and research indicate, there is a long way to go before contracts can be assumed to be understandable to all parties.

READABILITY OF CONTRACTS

Poorly written contracts heighten tense relationships between parties; especially in an environment where business competition is very intense. Management and labor are feeling the effects of compressed recessionary cycles. Businesses are only recently out of one downturn and are facing the prospects of another in a relatively short time period. Negotiations center on tough issues of work rules changes, management rights protection, and demands for concessions (Holoviak 1984). In this environment, disagreements over ambiguous contract language create more tension and distrust between negotiation parties.

In the last three years, there has been only a handful of research efforts investigating the ease of reading and understanding contracts. There have been few books written on the technical aspects of writing a contract. The few articles available have suggested that contracts are not easily used in the work environment (Suchan and Scott 1984). Supervisors, stewards, and other parties that must refer to the contract for guidance tend to be confused or cannot understand at all what the contract is supposed to be communicating.

In 1951, two separate research efforts, one by Lauer and Patterson and the other by Tiffen and Walsh, applied the Flesch reading ease formula to a number of contracts to determine how easy they were for the reader to understand. The Flesch formula is a reliable and commonly used measure in this area. The results of the separate tests concurred on findings. Both found that labor contracts were in the "very difficult to understand" range. In 1981, Samuel Walker used the Gunning Fog index on a case study of one small collective agreement to determine ease of understanding and readability, and found similar results. The Gunning Fog index is similar to the Flesch index and is another commonly used and reliable measure. In 1984, Suchan and Scott research updated and expanded the 1951 works by adding a third reliability formula and a wider sampling of contracts. The research concentrated on seniority, discipline, and grievance clauses. These were selected because of their presence in most all contracts, which provided a common denominator for measurement between widely divergent industries, occupations, et cetera. Second, these three clauses are ones that are crucial for both labor and management to understand.

The results of the Suchan and Scott research were dramatic. All of the various formulas produced similar results, showing that the seniority, discipline, and grievance clauses all fell in the "very difficult to read" category. The authors translated the scores to indicate that to feel at ease in understanding the clauses, a person must have a reading comprehension skill of no less than that of a college graduate (Suchan and Scott 1984). Recent statistics indicate that the majority of our shop stewards, first-line supervisors, and the rank and file employees would not fall into this category and thus would have a great deal of difficulty understanding the clauses. Research studies indicate the proportion of the labor force with some college training is 33.5 percent (Moore and Elkin 1983).

When the readability of each of the 588 clauses used in the research was examined, only one clause was in the easy-to-read category—and this clause was rated easy-to-read on only the Flesch index. All the rest (including the one clause as measured by other readability indices) were in the "very difficult to read" category. The Gunning Formula suggested the language of the typical contract would require a reader to have 19 years of education. In addition, many of the clauses had negative scores, which indicates they are virtually incomprehensible (Suchan and Scott 1984).

The above research suggests that the principal users of a contract are well-educated managers and attorneys. For years the principal texts and reference books have urged the use of attorneys in framing contract language. Certainly, this is a contributing factor, but not the whole reason behind the problem. In addition to a gross failure to take into consideration the actual probable users of the contracts, the wording was vague and ambiguous, the sentence structure was found to be poor, and the writers of the contracts failed to include input from the primary users of the contract.

Poor grammar, poor use of words, and other problems of similar nature can in part be attributed to the environmental factors involved in negotiating a contract. Time pressures, marathon bargaining, and the heavy nature of the sessions add to the problem. This topic is treated in some detail later in the chapter.

Failure to include the primary users of the document in the writings is as major a problem as the overreliance on attorneys. Some agree this is still a function of the use of attorneys; that is, writing so that arbitrators and other attorneys will understand if problems arise that require their interpretation. The fact remains that, for seniority, discipline, and grievance clauses, the principal users will be first-line supervisors and union stewards. Failure to include this group in the writing, or at least the review, of contract clause proposals is to abdicate the responsibility into the hands of attorneys.

TIPS FOR MORE UNDERSTANDABLE CONTRACTS

Gathering relevant input helps to avoid the unfavorable condition of incomprehensible contracts and need not be a complex process. Supervisors, union stewards, and rank and file employees with appropriate capabilities could be solicited for changes they desire to the collective agreement. This solicitation could include their offering a sample of how they would like the specific issue worded. Refinements to proper grammar could be made by the industrial relations staff. Review for legal ramifications, not rewriting, by company counsel is also possible. This is not unlike the movement to keep supervisors involved in the grievance process beyond the "step one" level by their writing the management response (with review by the industrial relations director). Many organizations currently solicit input from this group for issues and changes they would like to include in the contract. It would be a natural extension of this process to have contract items offered in sample form.

In many states, various loans to individuals through banks and financial institutions require the document to be written in laymen's terms. Technical and legal terms are replaced with vocabulary familiar to the reader, in language that is understandable, and in such a way that all pertinent aspects are disclosed to the reader. If steps can be made to delegalize the complex legal and financial language in a loan agreement, then certainly steps can be made to reduce these problems with collective agreements.

There are subscription services available that offer sample contract clauses and copies of contracts from various organizations. These services are all well presented in terms of the current state of the art with regard to each area covered. Unfortunately, the state of the art is too complex for the average user. To recommend further usage of such clauses will only perpetuate the problem and not lead to a solution. The solution will come about only when the primary people affected by each clause have sufficient written input and final review of agreed-to terms.

To offer an example, consider the following sub-clause taken from a grievance article dealing with time limits to complain: "If any complaint or grievance is not submitted or presented in accordance with the successive steps and within the procedure hereinbefore set forth in this Article, it shall be deemed settled unless a mutual waiver of time limits have been given by the parties."

The above clause is certainly not the worst case scenario of the type referred to earlier. Yet, it could be rewritten in a simplified manner. If nothing more, it could be written as more than one sentence. To illustrate, a simplified version might read as follows: "If an employee has a complaint or grievance, 'time limits' and proper procedures for steps described in this Article must be followed. If both are not followed, the complaint is considered settled (i.e., no longer exists). The only exception is if the parties involved agree to ignore the time limits."

THE INTENT OF THE PARTIES IN CONTRACT LANGUAGE

A key point in the analysis of any written agreement is that a person asked to interpret a clause should be able to judge what the parties meant at the time of negotiations (Elkouri and Elkouri 1973). The contract language should be broad enough to accomplish the desired end results. It should not be written narrowly and technically in an attempt to avoid problems or reduce grievance activity by its construction. It cannot be assumed that if contracts are constructed to remove issues of possible complaint, then there will be no complaints. Obviously, the complaints will surface, possibly marked in the technical language of another clause. Of more significance is the injury to the relationship of the worker and organization.

Arbitrators are frequently called upon to judge the intent of two parties where contract language is unclear. That is, they are called upon when reasonable yet conflicting arguments can be made by both parties as to proper interpretation. Decisions tend to be based on what the perceived goal of the parties was during the writing of the contract. The outcome is based on intent, not the reasonable interpretation of the language. The arbitrator will attempt to take the place of the parties at the time of negotiation to gain a grasp of the circumstances leading up to the written agreement. Such items as company and union newspapers or negotiations updates are often used by the arbitrator to gain both a feeling of the bargaining atmosphere and a flavor for the bargaining history of the parties. Where present, stenographic records are reviewed along with other pertinent documents. It should be noted that items such as the various counter proposals used to arrive at a settlement are not used, nor are any privileged communications. Oral testimony of people attending the negotiations will be accepted if other forms of evidence are lacking. The rule of intent is explained in the following quote:

> Whatever may be the inaccuracy of expression or inaptness of words used in an instrument in a legal view, if the intention of

the parties can be clearly discovered, the court will give effect to it and construe the words accordingly. It must not be supposed, however, that an attempt is made to ascertain the actual mental processes of the parties to a particular contract. The law presumes that the parties understood the input of their contract and that they had the intention which its terms manifest. It is not within the function of the judiciary to look outside the instrument to get at the intention of the parties and then to carry out that intention regardless of whether the instrument contains language sufficient to express it; but their sole duty is to find out what was meant by the language of the instrument. This language must be sufficient, when looked at in the light of such facts as the court is entitled to consider, to sustain whatever effect is given to the instrument (12 American Jurisprudence, 227).

If the words in the contract were clear and conveyed a single distinct interpretation, there would be no need for a background investigation. In such cases the arbitrator would be bound by clear intent of the parties, even if the results may be more severe than either side intended during the writing. To avoid the many problems faced in judging intent, attention to detail should be used in collective agreements.

AVOIDING AMBIGUOUS CLAUSES

Ambiguities in contracts exist for a wide variety of reasons. The reasons include purposeful ones to avoid direct conflict over what appear to be minor issues, those that result from time constraints, and excess use of legal counsel in phrasing of the language. The nature of language itself can create many problems; for instance, problems occur due to words that have multiple meanings, regional differences in the definitions and usage of words, and the connotative meanings of words that elicit different reactions in people.

During the negotiation of a collective agreement, details are worked out vocally and then set down in writing. The business of where the speaker accents a word or phrase, the loudness or pitch of the voice, and the intensity of emotion may all be lost when the words are set in shallow type on a page reconstructed in "proper" legal phrasing. From the bargaining table to printed contract in use, incredible gaps in meaning can result.

Sentence construction can result in significant confusion as to intent when used by supervisors or stewards, even though the meaning was clear during negotiations. To use a 1983 illustration by Paul Prasow and Edward Peters, "The mother was a small farmer's daughter." In this phrase, what is small? The mother? The farmer? The farm? Only the writers will ever know for sure.

Ambiguities may also result when words are not clearly defined. Words that on the surface may suggest a single meaning, may have multiple meanings and applications in usage. For example, the term "hours worked" during the year, which seems rather straightforward, has at least three frequently used definitions. Each of these definitions will produce different numbers. "Hours worked" may mean straight time hours worked, which refers to the typical 40 hour week for 52 hours or 2080 hours a year per employee. It may mean total productive hours worked, which would be 2080 hours minus all breaks and vacations. It could also mean total paid hours or 2080 plus all overtime, et cetera. Another example is use of the term "years" of service, on which sick leave and vacation eligibility are often based. Again, there are at least three common uses of the word "year" in a contract. There are calendar years, January 1 to December 31. There are seniority years, which are based on the anniversary date of employment. And there are contract years, which are based on the anniversary date of the collective agreement.

Clearly, without defining and specifying, perhaps adding qualifying words in the above examples, confusion is likely to result. Another form of confusion is referred to as latent ambiguity. Contracts have latent ambiguity when the language is clear, intelligible, and suggests only one meaning; yet, extrinsic facts or other evidence makes it subject to multiple interpretations. For example, the contract may tie wage rates of several key jobs to those paid at locally selected companies. On the surface this appears to be precise wording with only one possible interpretation. Yet, what if the job requirements vary greatly between the selected local companies and their company for the key jobs in question? The provision stipulating this arrangement becomes unenforceable.

WAYS TO WRITE CLAUSES TO AVOID PROBLEMS

Potential contract problems can be tactfully avoided, by keeping some "rules of thumb" in mind. These include many of the things learned in our secondary school grammar courses; such as avoiding words that may have more than one definition, trying to use specific versus general language, and avoiding the hazards of long, detailed clauses.

Many ambiguous and potentially difficult situations may be avoided, by using such items as coordinate structure of sentences. Our written language provides conjunctive forms for use as markers of parallelism in cases where one finds parallel elements. Use of conjunctive forms can prevent ambiguities (Prasow and Peters 1983). Forms like "either . . . or," "neither . . . nor," and "both . . . and" can be used to clarify clauses. Consider the following clause:

> An employee who does not work the day before the weekend or the day after the weekend, will not be paid double time for weekend work.

Interpretations of the above clause can range from the employee's working only the day before or the day after the weekend to having to work both days to collect double-time pay for weekend work. Certainly, when reading the clause to members of the bargaining team, all the proper accents and vocal tones were present. Parties were clear as to the meaning; however, writing for interpretation by others of what is in writing may produce confusion regarding what is meant. The simple use of conjunctions could have prevented this. To clarify, the parties should have written the clause to read as follows:

> An employee who does not work *both* the day before the weekend *and* the day after the weekend will not be paid double time for weekend work.

or:

> An employee who does not work *either* the day before the weekend *or* the day after the weekend will not be paid double time for weekend work.

The choice of wording above leaves little room for misinterpretation. Simple adjustments in grammar avoid the possibility of needing to use an expensive solution to resolve negotiated intent.

Another classic problem in writing agreements is the use of words or phrases that intrinsically contain multiple interpretations. The meaning of such words/phrases as "reasonable," "sufficient," "just cause," "justifiable reason," et cetera, will vary depending on who is interpreting it. Such disputes in meaning are frequently resolved by referring to local customs or the past practices of the parties. The extra effort on behalf of the writers to define or provide explanatory classification of such words or phrases would be most helpful. However, these words often creep into the contract and stay in the contract because neither party wished to make them an issue to be resolved in a win-lose situation at the table. Vagueness may be preferred for situations requiring individual, case-by-case decisions. Clearly, the parties themselves simply may not know the limits to give each word or phrase at the time of negotiation.

Despite the understandable rationalizations for the use of words and phrases containing multiple interpretations, the fact remains they cause confusion and very often place the parties in a position of needing a third party to interpret specific meaning.

One rule for interpretation by arbitrators is that specific language takes precedence over general language in a contract interpretation dispute. Specific language refers to the ability to place the language in a specific class or category. Specific should not mean perfect precision in writing, but that which removes vague and ambiguous points.

The language of the contract can be specific on an issue and still remain loosely written. Authors writing on this topic often caution against the use of specific language without due care and research. In an effort for protection against either losing managerial prerogative or being too soft on issues from the union perspective, negotiators often fight for specific language in specific sections of the collective agreement. The end result may be to preclude the arbitrator from using well-established case precedents that would be to one party's advantage.

There is more than one example of unions trying to control the use of subcontracting work by writing in specific language on that one topic. It should be understood that construction of the clause may allow for some discretion on the part of the arbitrator in interpreting the clause and rendering a judgment because of the language used in the clause. Similarly, managers trying to control holiday and sick leave abuse have written themselves into corners by forcing issues or definitions of abuse, realizing later they did not cover other types of abuse in the same area. When one attempts to specify all possibilities the arbitrator often perceives that omissions were intentional.

The inclusion of one or more items in a list to cover all possible contingencies is used frequently by both parties to avoid general interpretations of the clause. This is used, for example, by management negotiators who hope to prevent erosion of their management rights by having long, detailed management's rights clauses. However, this process is frequently taken by arbitrators to mean that there are no other exclusions (47LA654, 44LA1045). Some negotiators have attempted to cover this built-in trap by placing a general statement at the close of the list, hoping to include anything they may have overlooked. These general statements will be useful only to cover items of the same general nature or class listed before. If the item overlooked in the list of managerial rights is far afield from those listed, the statement will be held as useless (Elkouri and Elkouri 1973).

USE OF JOINT SUBCOMMITTEES

The use of joint committees in seeking the resolution of problems is increasing in modern organizations (Holoviak 1984). Such efforts as quality circles, safety committees, productivity improvement committees, and quality of work life committees, among others, currently exist. It would be natural to include problems in writing contract language as an effort for joint resolution within the committee process. The success of any committee resolution process depends to a great extent on the authority delegated and visible leadership support given to the effort. A committee to help write contracts would be no exception.

The joint committee would be useful over a wide spectrum of possibilities. These would range from simple review to actual writing of a clause. The review process would be helpful to catch mistakes in grammar and construction that would lead to ambiguities in hands of persons who must be asked to interpret the document on a daily basis, such as shop foremen and union stewards. Second, where detailed clauses have been negotiated, joint committees can be used to search for any key points overlooked or misworded in the midst of bargaining. For example, the subcommittee can review the company record book of discipline dispensed for various offenses over a given time period to ensure no inconsistencies with any points that may be detailed in the new contract. Third, where the tenets of basic agreement on an item are present between parties during negotiation, a subcommittee could be formed to complete the task of reading the agreement and hammering out a useful written clause. Fourth, joint subcommittees are helpful prior to official negotiations to begin the task of writing contracts in acceptable language—in a form and manner that can be understood by those who must read it and use it on a daily basis, not just the company counsel who may write it for protection from a possible court case in the future.

INTERNAL REVIEW

There are many practitioners and authors supporting the idea that both parties to a negotiation maintain some form of internal structure to review contract clauses prior to offering a draft to the other side as a negotiation proposal. The hoped-for result is to catch loopholes prior to negotiating the article, and if accepted, prior to implementation. It could be somewhat embarrassing to the management team to be negotiating a difficult subcontracting clause, only to learn in midsession the clause they desire has some serious loopholes present. It is too late to take it back at that point without alerting the union negotiators.

Internal review teams are often made up of the industrial relations manager, company counsel, and some middle-level managers. Certainly, the fact that an internal review team exists is positive, regardless of its makeup. However, the inclusion of a wider cross-section of managerial hierarchy, especially to include areas of proposed change, is more effective. There is no doubt that the wider the range in hierarchy and the more people included, the greater the resultant difficulty in confidentiality and the task of managing such a group. Yet, the input, especially from first line managers, regarding practical problems and other weaknesses can prove to be invaluable to the negotiation team. The inclusion of higher-level managers helps not only to gain support for the item but also to uncover potential difficulties in terms of organization policy or future organization plans of which the negotiation team is often unaware.

The union review team performs similar essential points for its own interest. With the union, review is often more necessary than for the management team. The amount of technical support available to local bargaining units depends on the size and wealth of the union. With the possibility of limited technical help, local bargaining units must use resources that are available to ensure contract demands they make do not work against them because of poor construction.

SUMMARY

A consistent theme throughout this work is to reduce the adversarial nature of the worker-manager-union relationship. The techniques vary with the topics of each chapter. The hoped-for result of a better written collective agreement is improved communications among the three parties.

Benefits of enhanced communications fill the pages of numerous books. Certainly the benefits extend far beyond reduced grievance levels and easier negotiations between parties. The suggestions for readability alone can make the collective agreement a more workable instrument in moving toward cooperation. If problems of semantics, ambiguity, clarity of intent, poor grammar, poor sentence structure, and intentional vagueness to avoid facing an issue are improved, so will the atmosphere of the labor setting. The people who use the document should be its authors. If special circumstances arise that will lead to the judiciary system, then the use of counsel may be required. With some practice and the application of a few points that have been discussed, the practitioner is likely to produce contracts that are significantly more effective than those currently in use. The optimum outcome would be to have the original intent of the whole industrial relations process simple enough in structure, apart from both the legal commercial contract form and the judiciary, to be useful in solving problems that arise.

11 Corrective Actions

INTRODUCTION

The necessity to take corrective action (discipline) with employees is faced in both union and nonunion settings. The particulars of the grievance machinery in the unionized setting will be discussed later in this chapter. However, the managerial skill to be learned is the same irrespective of formal union contract.

Disciplinary action normally takes place when employees violate the organization's rules or practices, or for such reasons as drug abuse, alcoholism, theft, and the like on the job. For the most part, people perceive discipline as a negative form of encounter. This is understandable with historic reference. During the eighteenth and nineteenth centuries, negative corrective action was the preferred course. In those times employees who were insubordinate may have had their tongues burned with hot iron, been whipped in the town square, or forced to wear a sign indicating the person was not a good employee (Stessin 1960).

Fortunately, legislation, the use of unions, and public sentiment have changed these harsh practices. Theory and emerging practice seem to consider discipline as a separate act from punishment. It is felt that any corrective action should be self-administered to whatever extent possible, thereby reducing the impact of the action on the employee's self-image and perceived self-worth (Huberman 1964).

Properly established personnel practices would ensure that the employee be aware of corrective options in advance;

that is, employees would be aware of the consequences of inappropriate behavior in advance. The choice then falls on the employee to select between appropriate behavior or inappropriate behaviors. The resultant corrective action of an inappropriate behavior is the employee's choice. The responsibility for discipline is now in the hands of the employee and not the supervisor. The implied point of view here is that corrective actions be systematic, clearly defined, and free of arbitrary supervisory actions.

RESTRICTIONS ON CORRECTIVE ACTION

Following in the same time period as the theory that employees assume responsibility for the consequences of their own behavior, there emerged various restrictions and limitations on management prerogative as to corrective action, including discharge.

The first of these involves the National Labor Relations Board (NLRB), which has the authority to reinstate employees with back pay if it is believed the discharge was the result of unfair action. And, since World War II, the use of arbitration to settle labor disputes has grown. Like the NLRB, an arbitrator may reinstate an employee with back pay if the arbitrator feels the discharge was an incorrect action. In fact, one survey concerning discharged employees found managerial action to be upheld only 42 percent of the time out of 400 decisions (Jennings and Walters 1976).

In addition, there is a growing body of federal legislation and judicial interpretation of these acts that presents other restrictions on managerial discretion. These range from the various amendments to the National Labor Relations Act; to the Equal Pay Act that requires equal pay for similar work and working conditions for both males and females; to the 1978 Pregnancy Discrimination Amendment to Title VII of the 1964 Civil Rights Act (Amended 1972), whereby equal treatment for all employment practices with regard to pregnancy, child birth, or related medical conditions are involved. These and other federal laws frequently encountered are described in Figure 11.1.

More recently, the right of an employer to unilaterally discharge "at will" an employee is undergoing dramatic change. Employees are asserting that they are entitled to greater job security. In certain cases, the monetary settlement awarded through judicial relief has been significant.

FIGURE 11.1. Federal Legislation Often Encountered by Personnel/Labor Practices

Legislation	Impact
1931 Davis-Bacon Act	Set requirement of prevailing wage rates for federal construction contractors.
1932 Norris-LaGuardia Act	Restrict use of injunction to prevent a strike.
1935 National Labor Relations Act (Wagner Act)	Intervention in labor-management matters by established employer unfair practices. Set minimum and overtime rates for government contractors.
1936 Walsh-Healy Act	Set minimum and overtime rates for government contractors.
1938 Fair Labor Standards Act as amended	Established minimum and overtime rates and time and one-half after 40 hours for all employers involved in interstate commerce.
1947 Taft-Hartley Act (amendment to National Labor Relations Act)	Allowed states to pass right-to-work laws, set unfair employee practices.
1959 Labor Management Reporting and Disclosure Act (Landrum-Griffin Act, amendment to National Labor Relations Act)	Gives employees more rights against union leaders. Established disclosure of union financial affairs.
1963 Equal Pay Act	Requires same pay for women as for men doing similar work under similar working conditions.
1964 Civil Rights Act 1972 Amended (Title VII)	Prohibits job discrimination based on race, color, religion, sex, or national origin.
1967 Age Discrimination in Employment Act Amended	Prohibits job discrimination based on age for persons between 40 to 70 years old.
1967 Veterans Reemployment Rights as amended (Military Selective Service Act)	Employer required to grant leaves of absence for military duty.
1970 Executive Order 11246	Federal contractors or subcontractors prohibited from job discrimination based on race, color, religion, or national origin.

FIGURE 11.1. (Continued) Federal Legislation Often Encountered by Personnel/Labor Practices

1970 Consumer Credit Protection Act	Set restrictions on discharge for garnishment of more than debt.
1970 Occupational Safety and Health Act	Employer involved in interstate commerce must comply with federal health and safety standards.
1973 Vocation Rehabilitation Act	Government contractors required to have affirmative action to employ and advance qualified handicapped workers.
1974 Vietnam Veterans Readjustment Assistance Act	Requires government contractors to have affirmative action to employ and advance qualified Vietnam-era veterans.
1978 Pregnancy Discrimination Amendment to Title VII	Equal treatment for all employment practices with respect to pregnancy, childbirth, or related medical conditions.

The basic doctrine of employment-at-will states that an employee may be discharged for whatever reason the employer may elect. In the past this doctrine could be changed only by statute or contractual agreement (collective bargaining or private).

The current trend of judicial renderings indicates there does not need to be a formal written contract to alter the at-will doctrine. Court cases in California, Washington, Michigan, and Pennsylvania have ruled that dismissals must be for "just cause" in nonunion settings. Also, an employee's tenure with the organization must be taken into account and employees are entitled to a fair hearing. In addition, such items as employee handbooks promising fair treatment, policy manuals that discuss equity, and hiring processes that include promises of fairness have all been used by courts to overturn at-will discharge decisions by employers (Bright, Weigle, and Holoviak 1984).

JUST CAUSE DISCHARGE

Considering the various federal and state laws, administrative agency decisions, and actions of the courts in wrongful discharge, deciding on a just-cause policy for termination is recommended. A policy that contains the following components will usually find judicial acceptance:

1) Clear and unequivocal forewarning of the consequences of behavior must be given to the employee. Generally, progressive discipline programs are acceptable. However, there are serious offenses where only one disciplinary violation is allowed; such as, striking a supervisor or major theft. This is satisfied by showing the only recourse for the employee is to dispute committing the violation. If it is concluded the employee is guilty, corrective action penalty is at the discretion of the organization.

2) The nature of the offense should be job-related. Only when outside activities impede the ability to conduct work performance can corrective action be taken. At that point, the just-cause is not the outside work activity but the poor performance.

3) Be careful not to violate the due process aspect of employee rights by poor investigation.

4) Administer corrective action in a uniform fashion. From the history of cases to date it appears a key in the court analysis is uniformity of rule application. Even if just-cause is present, the appearance of discrimination or bias, or retaliation against an employee usually will influence the court to decide in favor of the employee (Sovereign 1984).

As such, taking proper corrective action with employees may have significant impact on the organization. The subsequent topics discuss how to spot potential problems and to handle them in a fashion that offers guidance for effective discipline.

DISCIPLINE AND THE FIRST-LINE SUPERVISOR

The goal of any corrective action system is to have the problem settled as near the source as possible. In terms of unionized activity, this could be "step one" handling of problems. For companies that are not unionized, it will mean settlement between the first-line supervisor and the employee.

Generally, the first-line supervisor is the management representative most frequently involved in corrective action. In many cases the supervisor has trained the employee, helped form past practice in the defined work area, and been involved in the events resulting in some form of corrective action. To round out the typical scenario, the first-line supervisor will actually administer the corrective action.

Staff and higher-level managers will monitor the activities of the first-line supervisor. Personnel department managers will monitor to ensure compliance with company policy and change or reverse the action of the first-line supervisor only to avoid an arbitration hearing. Unfortunately, the reasons that upper-level managers reverse decisions are often not communicated to first-line supervisors. This lack of communication follow-through creates unnecessary tensions and can leave the first-line supervisor unsure of how to handle subsequent problems.

Knowledge of formal grievance procedures in unionized situations and company policies in nonunionized settings are important; but they offer little in the way of guidance in the adjustment of problems. The ability to deal with and settle complaints, grievances, and handle discipline is important for both the shop steward and the supervisor. The ultimate goal of any grievance/complaint handling arrangement is to settle problems (handle discipline) as quickly and close to the source as possible. In that light, the format suggested in Figure 11.2 is offered as a guide (Trotta 1976).

STEPS IN PRACTICAL HANDLING OF CORRECTIVE ACTION

Listening

The process begins with listening. This is probably the most important step to learn about taking corrective action and settling problems at the first-line supervisory level. The supervisor should be listening to detect underlying causes if the real problem is not brought out. At this step in the process, the supervisor should ask the employee to repeat the story. Research to date suggests that repeating a complaint, or an individual's perception of the story in a problem with the supervisor, will have a calming effect on the employee. This second telling of the story should be in complete detail. Listening has a major influence on the structure of and outcome from an interaction of this nature. Success is often contingent on the extent to which the supervisor really listens and pays attention to the employee (Wright and Taylor 1984).

Reduce the Tension

The next step in the process is to put the employee at ease. This was begun in step one with the repetition of the employee

FIGURE 11.2. Steps in Practical Handling of Corrective Action

Step	Explanation
1) Listening	Key to supervisory-employee interaction settlement. Be alert to hidden causes. Ask to have problem repeated.
2) Reduce Tension	Don't interrupt either of two statements regarding the problem. Don't argue or antagonize. All that may be needed is for the employee to vent pent-up emotion.
3) Detail Facts	Consider the employee viewpoint, take appropriate notes and ask logical questions.
4) Investigate	Poor investigation may lead to more problems later. Take necessary time and energy to check background information and employee side of story. Try to estimate what would be required to reach an equitable solution.
5) The Decision	Give the employee the benefit of the doubt. Admit mistakes, be forthright. If called for, administer discipline in line with the severity of the problem. Don't delay the process by passing the problem along to the next stage.

explanation. The effort now is concentrated on not interrupting the person during the two explanations. This involves not engaging in arguing or antagonizing the employee. This may be easier said than accomplished as some of the employee's points may be directed toward the supervisor. The purpose of a properly designed corrective action complaint handling system is to allow the employee the right of expression. A useful by-product of this in complaint handling is to allow the employee to vent aggression, which in some cases is all that may be needed. An employee who is very emotional and upset will not be capable of making an acceptable or rational contribution to the problem-solving process (Wright and Taylor 1984).

Detail the Facts

At this point in the process, the supervisor should ask logical questions, write down appropriate data and facts, and clear up any vague areas that remain. The supervisor should avoid any tendency to make snap judgments. To do so may violate the due process of the employee by failure to investigate. Consideration of the employee's viewpoint is critical in maintaining an attitude of critical good faith.

Investigate

Poor investigation of situations that will involve corrective action may lead to significant problems at a later stage in the process. Embarrassment at an arbitration hearing can be avoided with proper investigation. Poor or no investigation of the facts leading to snap decisions by supervisors may result in violating the due process rights of an employee. Where the basic notion of due process (fairness) by management has been violated, corrective action has been reversed. Specifically, in various situations, the failure of the employer to conduct reasonable inquiry or investigation prior to corrective action was a factor (possibly the sole factor) in the arbitrator's decision to refuse to uphold the discharge or discipline as assessed by management (Elkouri and Elkouri 1973).

Due process will go beyond just the investigation process. Most union contracts specify procedures for corrective action. Arbitrators will frequently refuse to sustain employer discipline action where they have not fulfilled the correct procedures specified by the contract. Usually the breech of procedure by the employer is not with specific malice against the employee, but rather, the problems frequently involve supervisors who are untrained in the proper techniques for handling corrective action. In these cases the supervisor may overlook/forget to do something, assume the guilt of an employee, fail to investigate, or fail to give the accused employee the opportunity to question the accuser.

The supervisor must distinguish between opinion and fact before reaching any decision in corrective action or complaint handling with an employee. Facts are truth that cannot be denied. An opinion is a conclusion or deduction that is open to other interpretation. If an employee complains about not being treated fairly in vacation scheduling, this is an opinion. The supervisor may respond that the schedule is fair; this again is an opinion. However, when the actual schedule for all employees is shown and the procedure for scheduling compared to this employee's schedule, that is fact.

Where appropriate, investigation should include gathering appropriate background information about the employee and the traditional disciplinary action used in similar situations. Certainly, a flawless record of a long-tenure employee is a factor taken into account, as would be the other extreme of consistently inappropriate employee behavior. Checking what type of discipline has been rendered in past cases of similar nature can avoid unnecessary embarrassment at an arbitration hearing and hurt feelings on behalf of supervisors when corrective action penalty is faced. If a supervisor renders discipline out of line with past practice, the probability of having it reduced in severity is a likely outcome. To be inconsistent in such matters would raise the possibility of discrimination charges. In similar fashion, it would be an embarrassing situation to be at an arbitration hearing and receive evidence of inconsistent administration of severity of discipline. To do so would in many instances result in losing the arbitration case.

The Decision

When all the necessary facts, opinions, and background information are assembled, a decision should be reached in a timely fashion; certainly not beyond limits specified in the contract. The goal is for the supervisor to be logical and fair. The process should not be delayed or passed on to the next stage in grievance procedure. And, the supervisor should be encouraged to admit mistakes if any were made.

The supervisor should at this point try to estimate what it would take to solve the problem at this level. The goal is to return an employee to a productive level. If either party feels the corrective action to be significantly biased, it will be an unacceptable long-term solution. In an adversarial environment, the desire to "win" must be suppressed in favor of sound logic and decision making. In similar reasoning, if there is a prejudice against the employee by the supervisor, this must also be suppressed.

Presenting the decision in corrective action situations needs to be handled with care, especially when the decision is unfavorable to the employee. In this situation, the supervisor should be considerate and help the employee avoid embarrassment where possible. The aspect of mutual good faith in this circumstance is essential.

When the decision is unfavorable to the employer, the supervisor must still use restraint. It is not uncommon for the employee to indicate he/she was right "all along," if only management had listened. When this occurs, the best advice is to have the supervisor be tactful and walk away in lieu of creating an on-going argument. Having managers at all levels be forthright in corrective action is essential. To respond to employees only when management is in the right, and to pass on problems to the next stage when wrong will result in their credibility being damaged.

POINTS IN PROPER DISCIPLINE

The prior discussions have alluded to various points in a correctly established disciplinary procedure. It is important to elaborate on the term progressive discipline. Progressive discipline involves more severe levels of disciplinary action. This is in line with the philosophy discussed earlier that suggests that the employer desires to alter the behavior of an employee to coincide with the standards set by the organization. For major infractions, such as theft, assaulting a supervisor, or failure to obey directions, the progressive line may be shortened.

The line of thought indicated by arbitrator decisions and in the decisions of various state-level human rights committees suggest that an employer should utilize a process of progressive corrective action (Elkouri and Elkouri 1973).

As opposed to the corrective action approach, the authoritarian approach for handling discipline may be used (Wheeler 1976). Authoritarian theory implies that the purpose of discipline is to punish and to serve as an example for other workers. The theory behind the authoritarian approach is that the punishment will serve as a vehicle to discourage further actions of this type. The authoritarian mode of discipline is being phased out by virtue of arbitrator decisions against such actions and societal pressure on state governments. To that end, it is hoped the pressure will quickly remove this from the organizational scene. The very idea of punishment has paternalistic overtures that most organizations with this management style are attempting to shed.

The typical sequence for the majority of rule violations in a progressive form of corrective action is depicted in Figure 11.3. The first step is normally an oral or verbal warning. In some cases there may be two times where the supervisor will attempt to correct improper behavior by verbal means. The next level of severity involves written warning. This should contain reference to the earlier attempted verbal or oral warn-

FIGURE 11.3. Levels of Progressive Corrective Action

Step Number and Name	Explanation
1) Verbal or Oral Warning	Supervisor speaks with worker about the problem. (This may involve two verbal warnings before proceeding to next step.)
2) Written Warning	Supervisor gives worker a written notice explaining history of undesired behavior. It should explain desired behavior changes and consequences of failure to comply. In some union settings this may be signed by employee. Additionally, if present, the "official" form should be used.
3) Suspension	If violation continues, a time period off the job without pay is prescribed. This is usually a two-step process beginning with one or three days off and progressing to one or two weeks off for continuation of undesirable behavior.
4) Discharge	If the undesirable behavior continues, the worker could be discharged.

ings. In addition, it should detail the behavior expected from the employee and the consequences of future violations.

The next level (sometimes two steps) involves suspension. This is a period of time away from work without pay due to continued rule violations. Frequently this is a one- or three-day suspension, and that will be followed by a longer time period of one or two weeks off without pay.

Finally, if violations persist, the employee could be discharged. This is the ultimate corrective action and used only when other attempts have met with failure. Note, this final level does not mean mandatory discharge. Some organizations have tried transfers to other departments, shifts, plants, or have recommended in-house counseling (Holoviak and Holoviak 1984). Progressive corrective action need not be confined to union settings. Contemporary human resource management theory indicates this to be a desired form irrespective of union influence.

ELEMENTS OF CORRECTIVE ACTION BROUGHT TOGETHER

Figure 11.4 brings together the various elements of corrective action where undesirable employee behavior patterns are involved. Corrective action is an involved process with both psychological and legal overtones. To be careless in the process will result in an ineffective system and possible legal ramifications.

The technical process in Figure 11.4 is to be carried out with the lessons discussed in the practical handling of corrective action that involved listening, tension reduction, detailing of facts, investigation, and decision making. The elements begin with clearly written rules and progress through enforcement, reliable evidence, utilization of progressive action, and implementation of the decision or mode of corrective action to stop the undesired behavior.

The need to be aware of the proper elements in a corrective action does not stop with the issuance of a penalty. Consideration must be given to any mitigating circumstances or extenuating facts surrounding the situation. It is not uncommon for the evidence to support the charge of wrongdoing, but have the management decision reversed because of special circumstances. In addition, the reasonableness of the penalty relative to the offense should be considered. Anything out of line with past practice or deemed to be too harsh or severe will be lowered in severity by an arbitrator.

PROCESS OF A GRIEVANCE

The typical grievance procedure used by organizations has evolved to its present state. It was not developed based on solid research regarding the optimum means to settle unresolved problems. As such, the actual procedure used by individual organizations varies significantly in detail. Furthermore, the collective aspect and volunteer initiative of arbitration clauses in contracts further magnifies the differences.

The actual grievance process begins if a problem is unresolved after the initial steps in practical handling of corrective action have been completed. That is, the initial process of discussion leaves the employee dissatisfied with the outcome. However, a grievance can be more than a complaint filed by an employee against management. It can also be a complaint filed by the union against management and by management against

FIGURE 11.4 Elements of Corrective Action

	Elements	Decision Point	
1)	Clearly Written and Reasonable Rules ↓ Yes ↓	→ No	If this basic element is lacking then there is a high probability of the worker being indicated as not guilty by an arbitrator.
2)	Are Behavioral Consequences of Rule Violation Explained to Employees ↓ Yes ↓	→ No	Employees need to realize what will happen as a result of continued undesirable behavior. It is not always safe to assume that having a procedure manual will be protection. Also, any rule changes, or decisions to enforce current rules must be adequately conveyed to workers.
3)	Consistency of Application ↓ Yes ↓	→ No	If there have been prior or subsequent cases where supervisors have not been consistent in application of rules and in handling of undesired behaviors, there exists a high probability the employee will be considered not guilty.
4)	Thorough Investigation and Proper Documentation ↓ Yes ↓	→ No	Proper investigation of actions and credible documented evidence is an essential part of the due process arrangement.
5)	Progressive Action ↓ Yes ↓	→ No	With the exception of actions of such a nature as to make other forms of discipline inadvisable, to ignore progressive action is to invite failure on behalf of management in its attempts to change undesired behavior.
6)	Convergence of Specific Action		When it is decided that a specific corrective action remedy is needed to change an undesired behavior the following items are important to consider. 1) Mitigating circumstances 2) Reasonableness of penalty in relation to the wrongdoing.

the employee or union. The latter is a rare occurrence. In any case, the complaints relate to terms and conditions of employment and are produced in written form.

The process received its real push into common usage with the War Labor Board in World War II. The theory was to use binding arbitration to avoid industrial strife that would upset the main war effort. Prior to this time, neither unions nor management were in favor of any program that put the individual party's fate in the hands of a third party.

Arbitration was selected and is considered the best mode of handling industrial disputes for a variety of reasons. First, through a series of court decisions it has been endorsed as more suitable than courts of general jurisdiction, and the decisions of arbitrators will remain, for the most part, unchallenged by the courts. The process is in theory less complex, cheaper, and quicker than courts of general jurisdiction.

"Cheaper" and "quicker" are relative terms. The traditional arbitration hearing costs well over two thousand dollars per side if split evenly between the parties, and takes over seven months from the date of a request for a list of arbitrators to choose from, to receiving the grievance award (Zalusky 1976).

In the second step of the process, both parties begin to work from the written complaint forms. Here additional parties may enter the process. The union side may have the grievance representative, a steward, and the management side an industrial relations representative. The discussions here will normally focus on the nature of the grievance relative to company precedent in prior experiences. If the problem remains unresolved, it will be moved on, with a management-written response, to step three.

At step three, the typical scenario is a conference meeting. The grievance committee, with top local officers, meets with the management committee, which will involve the manager of industrial relations and perhaps another company official (e.g., assistant plant manager). The conversation centers on discussing the grievance, with maximum input from both parties. The goal is to cut off the process and negotiate a settlement prior to arbitration. As such, the environment can resemble a plea bargaining session. It is not uncommon to trade-off other pending grievances at this point and perhaps settle several separate complaints.

Research indicates that trade-offs of grievances is not the most desirable manner of settlement, but it occurs quite frequently in reality. Unfortunately, not all the settlements that result from this step are satisfactory to other parties to the problem. The first-line supervisor who initiated the action may not be pleased with the negotiated changes to the disciplinary action. If the communications network back to the first-line supervisors is poor, it can result in their being discouraged and upset. It may actually result in the feelings of being powerless to discipline.

If the problem is still unresolved, many organizations have an intermediate step prior to arbitration. This will involve top union officials of the international representative and a ranking company official. This is a final attempt at agreement before leaving the discussion in the hands of a third party neutral (Figure 11.5).

FIGURE 11.5. Process of Steps in a Grievance Procedure

Step	Company Participation	Union Participation	Nature of Interaction
Step One	Foreman or Supervisor	Employee and Steward	Oral discussion of problem between parties. Usually practical steps in handling corrective action by management representative.
		[If problem is not resolved]	
Step Two	Manager of of Labor Relations	Local President or Chief Steward	Grievance put into writing. Two parties meet to try to resolve complaint. Management response put into writing.
		[If problem is not resolved]	
Step Three	Members Management Grievance Committee	Members Union Grievance Committee	Attempt to solve by negotiation of problems. Decision put in writing.
		[If problem is not resolved]	
Step Four (Not present in all contracts)	Top Ranking Management Official	Top Ranking Union Official or International Representative	Final attempt to reach a settlement prior to arbitration.
		[If problem is not resolved]	
Step Five Arbitration	Addition of a third party neutral to hear presentation of both sides.		Final decision binding on parties.

The final step is the arbitration hearing with final decision binding to both parties. The selection of the abitrator is spelled out in the contractual agreement, as are the limits to the arbitrator's authority. While the contract may detail a selection process, many organizations have a working method that is different from the agreed-to procedure. For example, the agreement may specify that the parties each cross off two names from a list of five, the remaining person to be the arbitrator. Yet, in practice they utilize an up-list of regularly used arbitrators.

It should be noted that in the prior discussion of the progression of the complaint through the steps no mention was made of time limits involved for receiving written answers. Limits vary among contracts and there is no prescribed amount. This is a negotiable item and can be arranged to suit the organizations and unions involved.

Somewhere in the neighborhood of 3 to 4 percent of grievances will end up in an arbitration hearing. That means that the bulk of complaints are settled in the steps leading to a hearing. Discussions with various practitioners, in the area of arbitration, provided a picture of how many complaints are resolved. Many persons in the field believe this figure could be enhanced by better training of first-line supervisors in the techniques of handling complaints. Second, if the supervisor is left out of the process directly after step one, the mistakes of the past will continually be repeated, or justification will result in passing complaints to later steps in the process for resolution. The supervisor should be encouraged to participate in the upper-level steps and put the step-two decision in writing, with necessary editing by the labor relations staff. It is believed this will help reduce the frustration encountered by lack of understanding about upper-step decisions and keep the supervisor involved in the process of reaching a workable solution. The most satisfactory solution possible is one worked out between the employee and the supervisor directly involved.

Step-two resolution rates range between 50 and 60 percent. Step three rates are 20 to 25 percent. There is only a modest rate of success at step four.

ARBITRATION DECISIONS

The arbitrator must be able to conduct the hearing in a professional and unbiased manner. As is the case in other aspects of labor relations, this process contains various elements of gamesmanship. For example, subtle references to past and future meetings between one of the parties and the arbitrator is used, hoping to send the opponent a message that they and the arbitrator are well acquainted and accustomed to working together. The games will also often include open histrionics to intimidate the other side and in some cases the arbitrator.

Both parties enter the hearing at a high emotional level, yet they manage to explain their stories to the arbitrator and try to discredit the story of the other side in the process. The arbitrator must have the skills and knowledge to keep the hearing orderly and objective for receiving and recording the evidence presented by both sides.

The decision of the arbitrator will be contained in a document submitted to both union and management sides. It will traditionally contain: 1) the statement of the issues; 2) facts about the case; 3) relevant contract provisions; 4) summary of each party's contentions; 5) the opinions of the arbitrator relative to case; and 6) the award, either grievance upheld, grievance denied, or some middle-of-the-road compromise (Holly and Jennings 1984). Some practitioners in the field do not put much weight on the opinion section of the document, feeling this is not a binding reaction and is unnecessary verbiage. Others feel it is important to a complete understanding of the case.

SUMMARY

An inevitable part of human resource management is taking corrective action. This results from violations of organization rules, or for such action as drug abuse, alcoholism, theft, and similar actions on the job.

An underlying theme of this chapter is that discipline doesn't have to be only negative in approach. Corrective action must be handled in a professional manner if the employee is to return to a state of high productivity.

To approach corrective action with only the intent to prepare for eventual dismissal of the employee is expensive. This means that many thousands of dollars may have been spent in training and preparing the employee to the current productive state. To discharge will require another significant investment in a new employee. This reduces the rate of return on invested funds and lowers productivity until the new employee is operating at a similar level of efficiency.

The chapter also instructed the reader on legal restrictions involving discipline and the various measures of "just cause" if discharge is warranted. A technique or model that the first-line supervisor can use to handle correction action is offered that includes safeguards to prevent violations of due process and the embarrassment of faulty investigation.

12 Formal Arbitration

INTRODUCTION

U.S. trade unions entered the decade of the 1980s with the greatest absolute numbers in membership ever. By 1978, the combination of union membership and employee associations totaled 22.8 million workers (Helfgott 1980). Much of the growth was due to the success of public unions and public sector civil service employee associations. The associations do not regard themselves as unions but do represent their members in contract negotiations.

However, union membership as a percentage of the total labor force has been declining since the peak reached between the mid-1940s and mid-1950s. Recent comparisons show the 1960 percentage of 31.5 percent dropped to 19.7 percent in 1978 (Helfgott 1980). Early data for 1980s suggest the decline will continue—to what level it is not certain.

The important point of the above discussions is that roughly one out of five workers is still a union member. This is significant enough a figure to merit time for handling the serious matter of arbitration hearings. Chapter 11 concentrated on handling corrective action, outlined the steps in a formal grievance system, and also alluded to various factors in arbitration hearings.

Increasing the odds for victory in arbitration is not intended to indicate a return to an adversarial posture against the union by the management group. It is important to note that the arbitration hearing process is set up to be adversarial in nature. This means the party with the burden of proof must present significant arguments on its behalf to avoid judgment against it. The notion of adversarial action by both sides should be limited by professionalism and preparation, not the use of personal invectives by cross-examination, reliance on argumentation versus evidence and facts, or excessive use of legal technicalities to tie up a hearing.

SELECTION OF AN ARBITRATOR

As mentioned briefly in Chapter 11, there are usually some criteria already in place to use for selection of an arbitrator. Many organizations may not follow the prescribed procedures in the contractual agreement, but rather follow an informal agreement as to the method of selection. Selection of an arbitrator will become more complex over the next decade as the bulk of the experienced group dating back to the War Labor Board era retires.

For many organizations, selection has become a comfortable process of using the same few persons on what amounts to a rotation basis. For many practitioners and researchers in the field, this period of transition from retiring old friends to finding replacements offers opportunities to move forward in this aspect of arbitration. It is no secret that the arbitration process was not designed on the basis of sound empirical research, but rather it has evolved over time with each contract varying with negotiated changes.

There are at least two key issues in the selection of an arbitrator or third party neutral: the nature of the issue involved and the background of the possible choices for selection. The nature of the issue involved indicates the parties involved should research the past cases for the possible choices for arbitrator. How many cases involving this issue has the person heard? In whose favor have they been resolved (management or labor)? Is there a key point that appears to be the deciding factor that shows up across the various prior cases?

Arbitrators are not bound by past case precedent to the extent present in the judicial system. Examining the choice of arbitrator by the nature of the issue will offer strong clues to probable success. That is, how does this case compare to those the person has heard previously? Is there a trend to decide in favor of one party or the other? If so, the person on the losing side of the issue will have to take a different approach from the way past cases were handled in order to win. This may or may not be possible. If the key factor(s) that appear across the various cases incline to the firm's benefit, then probability of success is enhanced by choosing the "usual" arbitrator(s).

The second issue, background, is approached from two viewpoints: 1) industry in which the person may have the predominant experience in hearing cases, and 2) educational training. Within an industry, there are similarities of customs usage and past practices that tend to prevail (Prasow and Peters 1983). For the most part, these tend to concentrate in areas other than operational aspects of the business, and generally are involved where the contract is silent on the issues. Similarly, repeated exposure to the same industry results in acquiring a familiarity with the working environment. An arbitrator who is not familiar with the industry is not automatically ineffective. Yet, it may be necessary to educate the person with respect to the particular organization, industry practices and, perhaps, to give the individual a tour of the facility so that the working environment can be visualized.

The educational background and training of an arbitrator is also an important factor in the selection process. Approximately half of the arbitrators are lawyers and the other half for the most part are persons with Ph.D.'s in Economics or Labor Relations. A large number of the Ph.D.'s are from a wide variety of backgrounds. There is an obvious positive side to having an arbitrator with legal training in the technicalities of the proceedings. The negative side to this is the possibility of overemphasizing procedural technicalities and the rigid adherence to "precedental" value of awards (Prasow and Peters 1983). Tying up the hearing with legal technicalities can hamper the intended simplicity of industrial arbitration. Likewise, overemphasis on contract criteria and consistency with past rulings will remove the arbitrational flexibility necessary to adapt to differences among organizations in an industry or among industries (Prasow and Peters 1983). Arbitration is not strictly judicial, but quasi-judicial in nature. Arbitrators should know when and how to deviate from the existing rules.

Educational background offers yet another avenue of thought in selection criteria. There is a line of reasoning offered by researchers that suggests that how an arbitrator decides is in part predicted on training and environment. The theory is that, if a person spends a considerable amount of formative adult life in college undergoing rigorous study in a specialized area, the end result will be a tendency to think and formulate attitudes in line with that discipline (Bankston 1976). That is, a person with legal training and a person with economic/labor relations training will view the issues in a different fashion, based on their training and the internalized value systems that accompany it. Bankston conducted considerable research into this theory and claimed there may be a difference in the outcome of cases based on different backgrounds of arbitrators (1976). The main types of cases were those of: 1) economic efficiency, 2) union involvement in management decision making, and 3) compulsory arbitration issues. His results showed economists/ labor relations-trained arbitrators viewed economic efficiency, union penetration, and managerial decision making as positive factors in decision making. Those with legal training found these to be of little importance in deciding an award. Lawyers tended to consider compulsory arbitration of issues to be important and valuable. The economists/labor relations group were opposed to the idea. In Bankston's view, this reflects the values associated with the training received (Bankston 1976).

There are other researchers who contend this is too simple a viewpoint. Yet, the feeling among many is that using the concept of matching case issues to individual arbitrator selection as another factor may give the selection process more validity.

The various selection criteria discussed above are intended to provide guidance. Certainly no one item should necessarily rule out a person. For example, if the trend of arbitrator decisions is not in the organization's favor (i.e., lopsided in favor of the other side), this may not indicate a biased person, but one who will decide the issue on merits and not think in terms of balancing a portfolio of decisions. The use of educational background is also a handy technique for selection of new arbitrators who do not have the case experience upon which to base selection.

PREPARING THE CASE FOR ARBITRATION

Thorough preparation for a hearing is of paramount importance. The goal of preparation is to end with a logical presentation of facts and evidence, and a witness that will construct a solid mental image of the case in the mind of the arbitrator.

Stating the Issue

Somewhere between the grievance procedure and the arbitration hearing, the issue to be resolved must be identified and agreed upon by the parties. Seldom is there a use of formal pleadings as in the courts. This would tend to upset the simplicity of the process.

If it is clearly worded, the grievance statement can serve as the issue statement. Unfortunately, in many instances it is not worded properly or clearly enough. During the pre-arbitration steps, the issue may be defined or at least developed in modified form. The parties may have been arguing for weeks and still not be able to agree. A fact frequently overlooked by parties who use temporary arbitrators is the unfamiliarity of the arbitrator with the early negotiations on this issue and the bargaining history of the two parties. For these reasons and for the purpose of defining the limits of arbitrator authority, the submission agreement is used.

The submission agreement written by the two parties specifies, in writing, the disputed issue by the use of question(s) to be answered by the arbitrator. In addition, it defines the authority of the arbitrator and procedures to be used governing the hearing and restriction on other matters the parties deem appropriate. This agreement is the important point of protection for the parties. The most common ground, under state and federal law, for vacating an arbitrator award is going beyond terms set forth in the submission agreement or the contract (Prasow and Peters 1983).

The key point is to strive for language that will weigh the argument in one's favor. It is not uncommon for a person to lose based on the way the submission agreement is worded. Past surveys of parties using submission agreements reveal the majority are able to reach a successful agreement on wording without undue debate over phraseology (Elkouri and Elkouri 1973).

Many cases come before arbitrators without submission agreements or a clearly defined statement of the issue (Prasow and Peters 1983). The arbitrator may call for discussion of the statements to clarify the issue and scope. Sometimes after the hearing is underway the arbitrator will offer an acceptable wording of the issue. If all else fails, the parties and the arbitrator proceed at their own peril.

Steps in Preparing for the Hearing

Presenting the case at the hearing does not require a person to be an attorney or possess a Ph.D. in labor relations. Rather, it requires careful and thorough preparation of evidence and arguments to be presented. As in many situations, a model or method to follow is often helpful. The following is offered as a guide to preparation for presentation that includes the essential elements to paint a clear "mental picture" of your case to the arbitrator:

1) *Review and Study.* The examination of the case history begins with Step One grievance input from the supervisor and progresses to the current point in time. This also includes review of the whole contract to see which clauses have an impact on the disputes and to compare to past contracts for changes in the clauses that are significant.

2) *Interview.* To get a full understanding of the case, talk to all people involved, being sure not to leave out witnesses for the other side. Give your witnesses an example of how to conduct themselves and how and what is involved in cross-examination. This will help them understand the relevancy of their testimony in relation to the whole case.

3) *Examine Evidence.* Gather the documents and statistical data that is expected to be used. Make copies for the other side and for use by the arbitrator. If the evidence is suitable, make pictorial exhibits (charts, graphs, drawings of the site, et cetera).

4) *Research.* Gather relevant precedent data on how similar cases were handled in the past from in-house sources. Check for any unwritten customs or traditions the other side may claim bears on the case. Research in one of the various commercial services past cases of similar nature to act as precedents. And, research the arbitrator's past decisions on similar cases.

5) *Outline.* The case outline should reflect the "flow of logic" of the case. Beginning with the opening statements, order of witnesses, evidence for introduction, and written arguments to support views as to proper interpretation of any disputed language. Witness testimony includes written questions and expected testimony to ensure key points are not left out. This practice tends to ensure a better understanding of the case, uncover weaknesses, test strategy, and display a well-organized presentation of the case.

Developing the Opening Statement

There is no rule that stipulates which party goes first in an arbitration hearing. Typically the grievant will go first, except in cases of discipline and discharge, where the company will present first. The union strategy is to counter their arguments. Yet, even these traditions may be changed. Any item in agreement between parties should be summarized in a submission agreement or some other document, not the opening statement.

A basic purpose of the opening statement is to frame in quick fashion for the arbitrator the differences between the parties as to the dispute involved. It is not the purpose to give detailed evidence, but to include an explanation of the important arguments that will be made with the actual case presentation. It should explain the pertinent contract clauses involved and refer to agreed-upon facts.

If the other party interrupts, you should object immediately and ask the arbitrator for the right to finish without such actions. The time for objections to statements will be afforded during the hearing, not at this juncture. If the other party is allowed to interrupt, the end of the hearing could take an unfavorable direction and could cause the presenting party to lose its continuity and diminish the impact of its statement.

EVIDENCE AND PROOF

If the rules for discussion of evidence were to be those applied in court proceedings, the discussion would be long, detailed, and complex. Fortunately, this is not the case in arbitration proceedings. There is basically only one rule concerning evidence submitted at the hearing. Any evidence is considered admissible that is pertinent to the case and helps the arbitrator understand and formulate a decision based on the issues.

The area of most risk for an award to be vacated by the courts is the refusal to accept evidence that might be considered relevant (Elkouri and Elkouri 1973). With this well established in various court cases, the rules of admissibility are liberal. This goes so far as to bear opinion, secondhand testimony, and hearsay evidence along with the more concrete factual data. For the person presenting a case it does not mean that one is relegated to sit idly by during the submission of what is felt to be questionable evidence.

The objection to certain evidence (e.g., hearsay), even if overruled, serves notice to the arbitrator to consider the challenge before giving it weight and to consider it in light of the whole record (Elkouri and Elkouri 1973). In similar fashion, witnesses should be allowed to proceed with testimony they feel is important, even when in technical terms it may be irrelevant. Such ventures into extraneous data may help the arbitrator understand the background, political considerations, and atmosphere of the relationship between the parties.

Burden of Proof

A frequent occurrence in an arbitration hearing is the direct conflict of witness testimony. If credibility of the witness is not an issue, then the arbitrator may allow hearsay evidence. This places the burden of proof on that party. The hearsay evidence acts to force the party to provide strong evidence to avoid a decision against them on the issue. This is not a "chance" declara-

tion against either party, but flows from the nature of the issue. The hearsay evidence typically will be placed with the
person where argument is further from the norm in a situation
(Maguire 1947). To illustrate, the normal break allowance is
10 minutes, and an employee uses 20 minutes. His explanation is that "the line supervisor said it is okay." The line supervisor delcares, "No, I said no exceptions to breaktime policy." If the credibility of the witnesses is not a factor to decide,
the burden will be placed on the employee. The norm in this
situation is 10 minutes. He took 20 minutes. To place the
burden on management would provide wide latitude for employees to make up stories for their actions and escape the consequences of their behavior by having the burden of proof fall
on management.

This burden of proof on each issue is called the "affirmative of the issue" and can shift back and forth during the hearing depending upon the nature of issues presented. In more
general terms, the burden of proof for the deciding issues will
rest with the party raising the matter. That is, the grievant is
required to prove the case, except in such matters as discharge
and discipline. In these areas, management is expected to produce sufficient evidence to substantiate its actions.

HANDLING WITNESSES

In the most basic form, the rule for handling witnesses is
to have them speak loud enough to be heard, clear enough to
be understood, and to tell what is known about the case. A common error among witnesses is to say what they think the arbitrator wants to hear—not lying, but trying to be helpful. This
delays and prolongs a hearing. Similarly, if they do not know
the answer to a question, they should simply say, "I don't
know." In putting together a case, it is advisable to meet with
the witnesses expected to be used. Question them as to their
ability to recall facts, and to remove the existence of bias and
self-interest. Attempt to resolve inconsistencies in facts relative to other witness's testimony. Examine the attitudes of the
witnesses toward the testimony. And, of course, try to ascertain
probable witness demeanor while testifying or any inclination
to maneuver testimony (Jones 1966). This review with the witness removes various factors that could damage the credibility
of the witness in the eyes of the arbitrator. This is not to indicate that the goal is to train the most convincing liars. It is

rather to ensure that such factors as voice modulation (e.g., speaking quietly when cross-examined), lengthy pauses in answering, and other factors such as those mentioned above do not damage the testimony of what may be a key witness. If asked during cross-examination if they received advice from their council about testimony, they should answer yes, and are not to be upset or distracted by this type of question. Any well-prepared person presenting a case will discuss the testimony of a witness in relationship to the whole case prior to the hearing.

There are at least two ways to handle direct examination. The witness can simply be asked to tell what happened. This would place the person on the stand in the position of being skilled enough to communicate the story in a clear, organized, and logical fashion. The second approach is to ask a planned set of questions to lead the witness through in logical fashion. This approach removes much of the stress from the witness and, if the answer is incomplete, the next question can address the issue until all the facts are brought out. The burden of communication skills will fall, perhaps appropriately, on the more experienced person asking the questions.

Large numbers of witnesses do not establish credibility or preponderance of evidence. Witness testimony unsupported by objective facts or lacking in objective evidence will not sway an arbitrator.

After witnesses have testified in direct examination, they may be cross-examined by the other party to the proceedings. This equal "right" cross-examination goes back to our Anglo-Saxon system of law. Often the opposing party will use what appear to be harsh tactics, demeaning inference, and aggressive vocal tones to try to impeach the testimony of the witness.

If the witness refuses to answer under cross-examination, then the entire direct examination is struck from the record. It is for these reasons as well that the prehearing review with witnesses is a necessary exercise.

There are a few helpful suggestions in cross-examining the other party's witnesses:

1) Do not cross-examine if the person does not say anything detrimental to your case.
2) If the answer or outcome of a cross-examination question is not fairly certain, then do not ask. "Fishing" for inconsistencies in the hope of impeaching the witness testimony may only result in their version of what happened being repeated. This

may have the effect of reinforcing its being perceived as the correct version (Siegal 1965).

It was indicated earlier that in discharge and discipline cases the burden of proof will ordinarily fall on management. As such, they frequently will go first in presenting witnesses and other evidence. A strategy criticized by arbitrators is for the other party to rely on burden of proof and base the entire case on cross-examination of witnesses, having no direct case (Elkouri and Elkouri 1973).

CLOSING ARGUMENTS

As a general rule the arbitrator will allow both parties to present closing arguments. Some arbitrators specifically request they have such arguments, and others may limit the amount of time dedicated to this. Closing summaries are particularly helpful where the issues are very technical.

These arguments should avoid the details of the case and concentrate on the key points. It should present a "flow of logic" of the parties' case. This can serve to paint a mental picture of the case, clarify issues for the arbitrator, and serve to assure the parties they have presented as complete a case as they are able.

BRIEFS

Closing statements and briefs will often serve the same purpose. Sometimes parties will desire to use both. More frequently, they will select one or the other. If the purpose is to present additional facts indicated during the course of the hearing, the brief may be required to complete the factual picture of the case for the arbitrator. However, there is usually a time limit for submission set by the arbitrator or agreed to by the parties.

It should be remembered that briefs will delay the decision further and could increase the cost. The trend in arbitration is to reduce the complexity, cost, and time delays. In some very formal settings, both pre- and post-hearing briefs are used. If it can be avoided, the record established at the hearing should be utilized for the decision.

SUMMARY

The culmination of a good complaint procedure for an employee is the right to a hearing before a neutral party who decides the issue. Despite the best efforts of management, differences of opinion will occur as will complaints on a wide variety of topics. A well-run procedure will settle most of the issues at step one in the procedure. However, some will need to be resolved by binding arbitration. To retain the integrity of the process and the faith of the employees in it, professionalism in all aspects of its handling is important.

The nature of arbitration is modeled after our court system. With that in mind, the adversarial nature of the system is understood. It is believed that by pursuing solutions in this fashion, the truth will be uncovered. To increase our odds of finding the truth, this chapter discussed key elements of the process.

The key elements began with careful selection of an arbitrator and offered various criteria such as fast case decisions, education, and background to look at for guidance. A second element was thorough preparation for the hearing. Other elements included technical items such as developing opening statements; handling evidence and proof; burden of proof; writing briefs; and preparing closing arguments. Finally, the sensitive, yet important techniques in handling witnesses included direct examination and helpful hints for cross examination such as not to cross-examine if nothing detrimental to your case is offered.

Poor preparation and handling of the formal arbitration process can lead to decisions by the arbitrator that can set precedents for future actions of management or labor that one may not wish to "live" with forever. In addition, arbitration is an expensive solution. To pursue this avenue without due intensity is to waste resources.

IV Making It Happen: Today and Tomorrow

This part is a key area to the success of the concept being offered by the authors. Chapter 13 does something no other book on our topic has ever tried, tackling the question of how to convince people within the organization to see and use the new human resource concepts. This chapter is based on sound internal marketing techniques that bear strong ties to the state of the art in this area.

Finally, Chapter 14 offers a vision of what will be happening in the fast-paced world of human resource management, based on the best research and opinions available, and it compares them with the concept offered in the book. The comparison lets human resource managers feel confident that, by following the suggestions of the authors, they will be able to handle the changes that will inevitably occur.

13 Marketing: The Heart of The Matter

INTRODUCTION

The reader might well question the inclusion of a marketing chapter in a book dealing with human productivity and optimization of the organization's investment in people. It is the authors' contention that understanding strategic marketing concepts, in a broad and specific sense, is essential for the attainment of organizational goals in human productivity and optimization of the organization's investment in people.

The American Marketing Association adopted a new definition of marketing in 1985 (the first change since 1960): "Marketing is the process of planning and executing the conception, pricing, promotion, and distribution of ideas, goods, and services, to create exchanges that satisfy individual and organizational objectives." This definition lends itself particularly well to being used as a basis for understanding the nature of marketing that takes place within a firm. Marketing that takes place within the organization is largely the marketing of ideas, often to the employees of the firm.

Traditionally, the marketing of these ideas has been discussed and examined within the context of how one motivates co-workers and employees. With the study of motivation comes the understanding that motivation is not something that can be done to someone—that people cannot control what other people do. People can control only their own actions, which can result in a desired response on the part of other people. This desired response can be obtained, in both the sale of an idea or a bar of soap, through effective marketing. This understanding will form the basis for the internal marketing concept, which will be developed throughout this chapter.

This chapter will propose a definition for the internal marketing concept. A discussion of general systems theory and exchange theory and a presentation of ideas that support a broad view of marketing and its potential applications will be followed by a discussion of strategic marketing and how it might be applied to the internal marketing situation. Areas for investigation will be suggested throughout. A presentation of the findings of current studies will follow, highlighting applications of marketing theories.

INTERNAL MARKETING

In order for management to perform effectively in attainment of organizational goals through optimization of its investments in human resources, it must assume a marketing orientation. The marketing concept developed by McCarthy (1984) provides a good framework for development of an internal marketing concept, which the authors would present as follows:

> The internal marketing concept suggests that management must assume an employee needs and desires orientation and utilize an integrated company effort in order to attain its organization's goals, usually profitability.

In the case of marketing a consumer good, such as soap, the logic of using the marketing concept is clear. It is easy to understand that the company is more likely to sell soap profitably if everyone works together to give the customer what the customer wants.

It should also be easy to translate that logic into the labor-management relationship. The company is more likely to achieve its organizational goal of optimization of the use of its resources (sometimes called maximum productivity—or profitability—or returns on investment) if everyone works together to attain these goals.

One thing that clearly makes internal marketing a unique marketing application is that both management and labor could benefit from perceiving themselves as marketers. While this is true, this chapter will concentrate on the effective application of marketing from managements' point of view in its relationship with labor.

One comparison that may highlight the importance of this discussion is that between consumerism and unionism. Peter Drucker is often cited as having suggested that consumerism is evidence that people are not using the marketing concept. "Consumerism is the shame of the marketing concept." Unionism is evidence that people have failed to utilize the logic of the internal marketing concept.

USES OF THEORY IN MARKETING

A brief outline of some theory underpinning marketing, including possible applications for internal marketing and examples of directions for further investigation, might help clarify this discussion and lend weight to the arguments for adopting a marketing orientation when handling human resources. General systems theory and exchange theory approaches are presented.

General Systems Theory of Marketing

Sirgy (1984) suggests that marketing should be reviewed from a general systems perspective. He has attempted in his work to synthesize social psychological principles into a general systems theory, which is then applied to marketing.

Sirgy presents marketing as a social system composed of two or more individuals interacting with each other in a manner different from their interactions with other individuals (Berrien 1968). He suggests that this social system is comprised of two conflicting components—a drive to satisfy individual needs and desires and a drive to satisfy the demands of the system as a whole. This can be seen in traditional marketing systems that utilize the marketing concept as function conflict. There is tension between the marketer and the consumer that results in the needs of both parties being met, therefore, meeting the goals of the system, e.g., the marketer provides what the consumer wants, the company stays in business at a profit, and the system is maintained.

This can also be seen in the management/labor system. Sirgy uses the examples of the management/labor conflict to illustrate his point.

> Management . . . strives for high productivity, efficiency, and meeting the demands of the organization at large or its shareholders whereas labor strives to satisfy its needs in terms of wages and other benefits. Adaptation or growth of the social system with its subsystem achieves satisfaction of its needs and goal states provided that it is successful in satisfying both

[sets of] . . . goals . . . Job satisfaction leads to job motivation and high performance; high performance serves to meet environmental demands, which, in turn, rewards the organization, generating greater satisfaction for its members.

Sirgy suggests that marketing, a social system, having progressed or matured through several "levels," including such areas as nonprofit and social marketing, is now in "Level Six, Marketing and General Systems Theory." This means that not only is marketing a suitable application for a general systems theory approach encompassing many theories such as those from social psychology, but also marketing as developed based on a general systems theory may be generalizable to other disciplines. Drawing on Bagozzi (1975), Sirgy states:

The next stage of the maturation of the marketing discipline involves the generalizability of marketing principles to other hierarchical social levels. Can marketing be conducted with or without an organization? Can two persons engage in marketing? Can two societies engage in marketing? Can we talk about marketing between or among social entities?

Keeping these thoughts in mind, consider Bagozzi's thoughts on marketing—exchange.

Exchange

Bagozzi (1975) has suggested that marketing theory concerns itself with two things:

1) Why do people and organizations engage in exchange relationships?
2) How are exchanges created, resolved, or avoided?

He suggests that exchange is "more than the mere transfer of a product or service for money," and that "the reasons behind the exchange—the explanation of its occurrence—lie in the social and psychological significance of the experiences, feelings, and meanings of the parties in the exchange." Bagozzi goes on to suggest that exchanges can be utilitarian, symbolic, or a mixture of the two.

Utilitarian exchanges are those that involve giving goods for money or other goods and that "the motivation behind the actions lies in the anticipated use or tangible characteristics commonly associated with the objects in the exchange." Symbolic exchange involves the exchange of "intangible entities" such as psychological or social meanings.

Clearly, we accept the above as being true of exchanges in a traditional marketing situation. In the case of a bottle of perfume, the individual is willing to give up money in order to gain certain intangible social and psychological objectives and in anticipation of the use of the perfume. The marketer is willing to provide the perfume in anticipation of the use of the money exchanged for it.

Sheth and Gardner (1982) suggest that the concept of economic exchange is being replaced with the concept of exchange of value. This balances the power between the parties involved in exchange.

What is interesting is the application of these ideas directly to the management/labor situation, especially when viewed in conjunction with the understanding of this relationship as a social system. One can assume that it is in the best interests of both management and labor to maintain the system—to stay in business. It is important, then, to understand that there is exchange taking place within the system. Management and labor are both giving up and gaining something of value within the social system of the organization. They are both investing resources in order to achieve the organization's goals—in order to stay in business profitably. Management is giving labor money, benefits, and quality of work life in exchange for productivity, loyalty, and the resultant return on investment.

STRATEGIC MARKETING

Before going into depth regarding strategic marketing and its possible applications in the management/labor situation, it is important to note that it is not the authors' intention to discount in any sense the body of knowledge in management developed along traditional lines to manage human resources effectively. Rather, the authors are suggesting a framework or "general system" into which that body of knowledge can be integrated. Bagozzi (1975) puts it well when he states:

> It is not so much the fact that the subject matter of marketing overlaps with that of other disciplines as it is that the problems of marketing are universal. In answer to Bartel's query, "Is marketing a specific function with general applicability or a general function that is specifically applied?"—one may state that it is neither. Rather, marketing is a general function of universal applicability. It is the discipline of exchange behavior, and it deals with problems related to this behavior.

We are assuming in this work that the principles of effective marketing can be applied to the internal workings of the firm. Following is a brief description of what steps to take for effective marketing, examples of how they might be applied in the management/labor relationship, and certain specific suggestions for further research.

Steps in Effective Marketing

The steps for effective strategic marketing include the following:

1) Identify a viable target market.
2) Develop a program to meet the needs of the target market you have identified.
3) Implement and evaluate the program you have developed.

The above steps are guided by the marketing concept, which dictates a customer needs and wants orientation backed by an integrated effort in order to meet the objectives of the firm. In the case of the internal marketing concept, management would be concerned with employee needs and wants orientation backed by an integrated company effort in order to meet the objectives of the firm.

Identification of a viable target market requires several things. In order to be viable, a target market must evidence adequate potential. This potential is measured by whether or not these people evidence an identifiable need, whether or not they can be reached, and whether or not they have the resources to make the desired purchase.

This concept translates into the management/labor situation quite smoothly. Management must find people in the workplace who want to work, can be recruited, and have the necessary abilities to do the work required.

Identification of a viable target market also requires that the marketer understand the characteristics of the target market. In marketing, this includes who they are, how they behave, and what influences their behavior. These characteristics are sometimes referred to as segmentation variables and include such items as demographics; socioeconomic data; geographic location; activities, interests, and opinions; attitudes; sources of influence; and psychographic information. These characteristics help marketers identify the needs of individuals and how to meet these needs.

This can also be translated into the management/labor situation and is one of the many areas where research can be done to establish understanding of the variables involved. One example of possible usefulness of this understanding would be that a worker who is 25 years old and single may desire different benefits from a worker who is 40 years old with a husband and two children. A woman starting out her career later in life may have different needs in the workplace with respect to quality of worklife from those of a younger woman just out of school.

Another type of segmentation variable that would be important for management to understand in disseminating its ideas is the stage in the adoption process. People adopt products and ideas at different rates. Some are early adopters and some lag behind the crowd. Management can use this understanding to identify who would be most receptive to new ideas and who the opinion leaders are for the group.

Understanding the characteristics of labor with respect to as many different salient variables as possible can lend insight to management that will lead to maximum job satisfaction, productivity, and optimization of utilization of the organization's human resources.

Research should be done to identify salient variables and to develop a mechanism for segmentation within the human resources environment. It will be useful to management to reorganize its thoughts into a system that recognizes and builds on the line of thought that stems from marketing segmentation theory. This will lend depth and insight into the picture that management has of labor and will allow management to tap that resource more effectively—to sell its ideas to labor in return for maximum productivity.

Once the characteristics of the target market have been identified, including its needs and wants, a program is developed to meet those needs and wants. It is in this way that the objectives of the firm are met. For example, in a traditional marketing situation, the target market may express a need for a fuel-efficient car that is relatively low in price and looks sporty. Research indicates that this group is young, male, urban, low in socioeconomic status, watches no television, and is extroverted. The company can develop an offering to meet the needs of this group if it feels it evidences potential. If it evidences adequate potential, providing an offering the group desires will result in sales and the attendant profitability.

These principles can be applied as internal marketing in the management/labor situations. Management must make every attempt to provide an offering to labor that genuinely addresses the needs and desires of the workers. *This is the only way the firm can optimize its utilization of its human resources.* And it is the *best* way for the firm to meet its objectives.

Engel, Blackwell, and Miniard (1986) have said "understanding consumer motivation and behavior is not an option—it is an absolute necessity for competitive survival." This is true also with respect to understanding labor. Preceding chapters have described in detail the cost to individual companies and to the economy of workers who are not producing—of absenteeism and of turnover, for example. Labor's productivity can be earned by management. Management can sell productivity to the workers; but only through good internal marketing, only through exchanging something of value for something of value.

Perhaps the target market management has identified is recent high school graduates; capable but not interested in college; male and female; interested in jobs that pay well and allow them free time; and currently unconcerned with such issues as career path advancement and long-run job security. Management would do well to emphasize good pay and flextime, deferring offers of retirement benefits and career planning until these individuals move into the next stage of their life cycle. Another group may be most interested in job security, and be willing to give up flexibility or pay in order to attain it. Understanding the needs of different groups of workers allows management to offer specifically what workers want and need. This results in workers who are more likely to be productive—to give something of value in exchange for what they actually value.

The program offered in marketing has very definite characteristics. Again borrowing from McCarthy (1984), the marketing program or offering traditionally consists of product, place, price, and promotion, commonly called the "4 P's." Each of these elements is designed to work with the other elements to meet the needs of the target market and to, therefore, meet the objectives of the organization. In the above example, the young male urbanite, low in socioeconomic status, who does not watch television and is extroverted, has expressed a need for a fuel-efficient car that is relatively low in price and looks sporty.

Provided that there is a group of individuals with these characteristics that evidences adequate potential, the organization will meet its objectives, will make money if it offers this group the right product, at the right place, at the right price, and promotes it effectively. "Right" implies what the people really want.

The right product means not only the tangible car but the car that meets the core benefit sought by the individual, which may be status or excitement in addition to fuel economy. The right place may mean a local dealer or it may mean the individual would be willing to travel to a distant distributor if it means a lower price. The right price will reflect what the individual is willing to give up in exchange, but it also may contain elements of how easy it is to arrange payment or the way that the price affects the individual's perception of the long-run durability of the car. And the right promotion is the promotion or communication that will reach the individual, be processed, and be acted upon. If the individual does not watch television, wants excitement, and lives in Maryland, a television ad featuring a happy, calm, elderly couple buying a car from a dealer in Michigan is not going to result in effective promotion. Promotion, or communication, must be managed effectively.

There is an offering that management makes to labor in exchange for its productivity, loyalty, and the attendant profitability. This offering also consists of product, place, price, and promotion, and must be managed effectively. Specification of the exact variables involved in developing these offerings for identified target groups is an area for more definitive research.

One example of how the product aspect of the offering can be tailored to meet the needs of the employees would be the offering of cafeteria benefit plans, which allow the individual to choose the benefits desired. This might allow the individual who does not plan to have children to choose additional vacation time rather than maternity benefits. Perhaps day-care could be made available. Perhaps the individual is interested in career development, training, and job security. These desires should be identified and addressed.

Price includes what the individual worker is willing to exchange for the totality of the product received. For example, the worker may be willing to exchange productivity, loyalty, and talent for job satisfaction and job security. The exact nature of the price the worker is willing to exchange will change depending on the needs of the worker and the level to which those needs will be met.

Place needs may include desired variations in work hours, such as flextime, or in work environment, parking, or transfer possibilities. These can be found in conjunction with productivity as providing the values or satisfaction for which the individual is willing to exchange productivity, loyalty, et cetera.

Promotion is concerned with communication among groups of people and between individuals and is key in effecting exchange. Adequate communication within the firm through such mechanisms as quality circles may meet some of these needs in the work force. An in-house publication or organized social activities may also be called for here.

Clearly, these applications of internal marketing theory will need to be described more specifically through further research. Management must use a marketing orientation that acknowledges the importance of developing offerings that contain appropriate mixtures of these elements to meet the needs of the target groups effectively. This activity will result in optimization of the organization's investment in its human resources—maximum productivity and loyalty, for example—and the attendant attainment of the organization's goals.

PRACTICAL FEEDBACK

Certain organizations have followed these principles, though they have not necessarily understood that was what they were doing. The results, as reported in conversations with practitioners through focus group interviews, have been impressive. To illustrate, one company has successfully integrated hourly employees into active participation in the hiring process. The personnel office screens candidates for job openings to satisfy the union and the legal requirements. The candidates are then sent to the area of the job opening to meet with the workers. The hourly employees interview and make hiring recommendations. The experiment so far has produced very positive results, as it fills the needs of the hourly employees. Not only do they feel involved, they also are able to choose a co-worker with whom they can work effectively. The hourly employees feel a commitment to help the new employee be successful. They help in training and give tips on doing the job. This has resulted in dramatically reduced turnover for people hired in this fashion. In addition, the worker group has evidenced reduced absenteeism, tardiness, and grievance rates.

Many managers consider quality of worklife and quality circles to be just another fad. Focus group participants and research on the topic suggest something quite different. It appears that where participatory management techniques have failed, as shown, limited success is the fault of management. This is true because utilization of quality circles is not adopted as the new managerial style, but neatly inserted in the existing structure. Management is often going through the motions rather than responding to a genuine need on the part of the workers for increased involvement in decision making. It was refreshing to hear the number of companies with well-devised, well-supported plans that are achieving this participatory state of management. These companies have been astute enough to acknowledge that attitudes of line supervisors and upper-level managers would have a major impact on the success or failure of the programs. They have remained committed to the belief that the philosophy encouraging participatory management must ultimately prevail, and are moving along at a pace where the changes will be successful. As one corporate executive indicated, "after 85 years of authoritative management leadership, changing to participative management will take time and effort." But these companies see the good effects of implementing these programs on the productivity of the employees and, subsequently, the bottom line. Not only are the employees more committed to the work at hand, but they also understand better what that work is.

Another example is sharing information with workers regarding the performance of the firm, costs of raw materials, competition's performance, market share, and proposed reinvestment of profits in the company. The assumptions implicit in withholding that information in the past included such things as the assumption that the workers could not understand the information, or maybe they would somehow use it against the company. Clearly, the worker cannot commit and cannot really understand his work without adequate information. Workers need information. And, conversely, adequate information helps workers understand better what contributions their jobs make and how what they are doing fits into achieving the system's or organization's goals.

The cases reported to the authors via interviews, focus-group actions, and in available literature support the positive effects of information sharing. Many human resource managers report the buildup to information sharing to be as exciting as the actual process. Companies report the workers feel better about knowing the information about the product they help produce and better understand the economic implications of their actions. At the bargaining table, companies are forced to be more professional and precise because of disclosure of data; no fault can be found with that. And, many workers respond positively when they understand what is needed in order to keep the company competitive and financially healthy.

The above actions on the part of enlightened managers toward participative management reflect good internal marketing. They would not talk about their actions as internal marketing and might well not understand the extent to which they have used a marketing orientation in order to achieve their organizational goals.

Several companies have been successful in a short-run sense, not because they used good strategic marketing principles, but rather because they were lucky. Atari and Texas Instruments are examples of this. They tried to keep going without a solid framework and failed. Both companies have hired marketers to lead them back to a more consistently successful path.

Businesses have come to understand that an effective marketing orientation—good strategic marketing principles—results in consistent, long-run business success. While managers may be realizing isolated successes with marketing-oriented techniques, they are likely to find that utilization of guidelines provided by a strong internal marketing framework in managing human resources will result in long-term, consistent attainment of organizational goals.

SUMMARY

The thoughts offered in this chapter are the tip of the proverbial iceberg. The framework that can be developed using the internal marketing concept is one that will be useful to practitioners in the area of management/labor relations. Internal marketing, when viewed as an exchange process within a social system, can be used effectively by management to identify and meet the needs of labor in order to meet organizational goals in the areas of human productivity and optimization of the organization's investment in people, and therefore, to meet the objectives of the firm.

This approach provides a truly fertile area for research in order to further describe and refine the definition of elements contained within the framework, and the framework itself. This research should provide a rich harvest for people interested in investing in others in order to achieve their mutual goals.

14　Future Trends

In the very near future, a major milestone will occur, one that it is very unlikely any of us shall see again. This event is the turning into a new century, year 2000. For the most part the year 2000 promises to be an exciting one. People growing up in recent times have realized opportunities afforded to few in history. They have seen the demise of the horse and carriage and the landing of a man on the moon. What the future holds is yet to be seen, but people can draw from past and present experience the knowledge that today holds the key for a better tomorrow. And this also holds true for the field of human resource management. Tremendous growth has been witnessed. At the turn of the twentieth century, organizations had no formal unit called personnel. What existed, if anything, was a paper-pushing position, recording vacation schedules and company picnic events. Today, there is a major shift in personnel. Even its name has changed to reflect its importance in organizations. "Human resource management" is finally getting its due position in the organization. And this is only the beginning. The last part of this century and the year 2000 promise to bring even more important developments in human resource management.

As for labor relations, there is no need to repeat its history here. It is quite evident that, in the early 1900s, organized labor had problems. These problems stemmed from the societal resistance to unionism. Businesses, governments, and the majority in society worked very hard to ensure a union-free environment. This "work" involved much bloodshed. While unionism is much more prevalent today, some resistance to organized labor still exists. The late 1970s were quite tumultuous and left people wondering just exactly what the nature of unions was. Concessionary bargaining was the norm in the late 1970s and early 1980s. Then it began to appear that labor/management relationships had gone full circle, and were heading back toward confrontation as many industries all but went out of existence due to labor/management difficulties.

The purpose of this chapter is not to dispute nor recount what has happened. It is, instead, one of predicting what may occur in the year 2000. No claims are made to having a "crystal ball," but it is suggested that, with some insight from the past and some deep thought, expectations can be generated. People have looked at the past, lived the present, and have generated a "think tank" of possibilities of what may occur in the future.

To accomplish this task, four global topics are going to be examined: human resource management; labor contracts; selling of companies; and where the labor/management relationship is going.

HUMAN RESOURCE MANAGEMENT

As noted above, the field of human resource management has changed drastically in the past 20 years. Its role in organizations and its function of providing superior service to the organization has increased. Most large companies are placing greater emphasis on human resource management, for many see this as a vital link in achieving greater productivity.

If the literature of the past few years is explored, focusing on the "best sellers" in the field, a list of books that have a common thread can be identified: valuing human resources. This value does not mean paying only casual attention to how much human resources mean to an organization; it means having a culture where it is commonplace to voice opinions, commonplace to develop one's potential, and commonplace to be properly treated. It is in these directions that we expect human resource management to expand, as these are directions that will produce symbiosis in the labor/management relationship and result in maximum utilization of resources and productivity.

Developing the culture that fosters the ideas above does not occur overnight. The process necessary to effect the change is lengthy and must be ongoing. Human resource managers will be pivotal in developing that culture. To achieve such a goal, human resource managers are going to have to take on new perspectives and embark on new courses of action. This means cleaning up the laxities that may exist. Jobs will need to be reevaluated to ensure that similar jobs within the organization are paid similar wages. Companies will need to embark on sophisticated human resource planning systems. These systems will be coupled with the career development process of the organization. As organizations trim down in size, human resource planning and career development will become paramount. Survival of some companies may hinge on this "succession" plan being in place.

Communications must also receive emphasis. Fostering a culture where human resources are valued must include a process of ensuring that adequate channels of communications exist. Employees need to know what is going on in the organization. Lessening communication lessens commitment, which will ultimately lessen productivity. Issues of concern must be made public. Employees are going to demand greater participation in decisions that affect them. One by-product of developing processes to facilitate this action will be a more committed work force. Increase commitment and you will increase productivity.

In addition, training and development must be considered. Training and development departments are likely to emerge as the most important component of human resource management. Why? Because to change an organization's culture requires changes in employees' behaviors. Making these changes usually cannot occur automatically. Changes need to be learned. And learning is corollary to training. For years, training and development was a luxury. As budgets got tight, training got cut. This will no longer be the case.

Skilled trainers, or change agents, will be increasingly in demand in organizations. These people will work closely with upper-level management to ensure the culture supports the strategic direction of the organization. These trainers will probably become a vital part of the organization's planning process.

The issue of culture in organizations (as described in terms of human resource planning, communications, and training) is going to bring about drastic changes in the daily activities of human resource management. This change will increase not only the efficacy of the function, but also its complexity. As such, the computerization of the human resource function is likely to grow rapidly. The proponents of change are going to need to make some changes themselves. Computer knowledge is likely to be one area for these changes, as it will probably become a requirement for jobs in personnel.

LABOR CONTRACTS

Negotiating labor contracts has also changed over the past three decades. Not only has the manner in which contracts are negotiated changed, but also the contents of the contracts have changed. Many years ago a "we-they," or "win-lose" mindset predominated. For we (unions) to get more, they (management) had to give it up, and vice versa, depending on the point of view. This win-lose situation gave rise to the confrontational mode of negotiating. While it would be wrong to suggest the confrontational mode of negotiating has ended, one can state that both sides have become more sophisticated in negotiation tactics, which has somewhat reduced the hostility that has been characteristic of these exchanges.

For instance, those negotiating the contract tend to be well trained in negotiation skills. This training is obtained through formalized schooling in labor law, industrial relations, etc.; or through workshops, both in-house and external to the organization. The psychology of negotiating, or understanding your "worthy opponent," is becoming more prominent in today's negotiations. More and more emphasis is being placed on achieving one's goals, more so than on the egos of the individuals involved. This aspect alone is expected to continue well into the future.

The mere fact that adversary relationships often do not produce the best results is evident. There is a good probability that both union leaders and management personnel will become more collaborative in their negotiation efforts. There is a growing awareness, which is being fostered by better flows of information in many companies that everyone working within the company has the same goals, is on the same side, and that the "enemy" is the competition—not the labor management. This is not to indicate that either side will always say "yes." It does indicate that both sides are maturing in their relationships. That maturity will foster improved relations and a more focused, integrated effort.

The second issue in labor contracts is the context. Both sides are required by law to negotiate wages, hours, terms and conditions of employment, and grievance procedures. There is no indication that these issues will cease to be mandatory bargaining items; however, who pays some of the bills may change.

We expect major revisions in health care offerings to union employees. Future negotiations are going to explore new ways of offering health care benefits to union employees so that costs in the health care industry can be contained. This is of concern for all organizations. It will not be settled by either side, but brought about by a consensus decision of the parties involved.

It is also likely that there will be a significant reduction in cost-of-living adjustments. There is a real move to the pay increases only to productivity, as tying them to other variables may lead to future problems. Organizations experienced many problems with COLAs in the mid-1970s, and more than likely will resist agreeing to COLAs in future contracts. Both sides, too, are becoming more cognizant that corporate survival depends on increasing productivity and/or its efficiency. Efforts to find ways to achieve this, including providing monetary incentives, will continue.

Finally, there is some indication that contract administration will align itself closely with the strategic operations of the organizations. As significant changes are made (e.g., automation), provisions in the contract will set into place how these changes can be made such that their impact on the workers is minimized. This may result in provisions on retraining, job bidding, and job classifications.

SELLING OF COMPANIES

In this section, we'll explore two themes: bankruptcies and plant closings. Without a doubt, the past ten years have caused a major change in our labor relations environment. The number of plant closings, companies filing for bankruptcy, and the residual laying off of union members has made almost every major newspaper's headlines. We saw that in the mid-1980s the Supreme Court ruled that a company could eliminate its mandatory relationship with a union by filing for bankruptcy. This action, while it dealt a severe blow to labor relations, has not, however, materialized into a standard operating practice.

What has occurred, with devastating results, is that many of our industrial plants have closed. The once strong "smoke-stack" industries have been hard hit by management and marketing incompetence, past inflation, and continuing foreign competition. As these were the strongholds of unionism, the result has been a tremendous decrease in the number of employees employed in those industries and has led to a decline in the unionization of the workforce. In fact, while the overall percentage of the workforce that is unionized has decreased for a couple of decades, it was not until the early 1980s that the actual number of card-carrying union members declined. This has been almost unprecedented in modern labor history. So where do the filing of bankruptcy and plant closings leave union members in the next decade?

First of all, the economics of running a business are "facts of life." Those organizations that cannot remain competitive will go out of business. There is going to be a more concerted effort on the part of unions and management to stave off this happening. As mentioned earlier, many of the past practices of labor and management will change significantly. Among other things, there is likely to be a significant increase in the use of quality circles, giving the workforce more say in its daily work. It is, after all, the workers who will make or break the organization ultimately, not management. Participatory management is a proven means to increase efficiencies in production. Unless commitment to efficient production is the standard, survival of the organization is in jeopardy. For instance, consider steel companies where employees have a vital role, or for that fact, where the employees have actually purchased the businesses. These have proven to be successful businesses. The success can be attributed to many things, certainly including the workers' commitment and subsequent efficient productivity. While many organizations have in the past paid casual attention to quasi quality circles, and then abandoned them, organizations in the future can be expected to use them to a greater extent. Whether it is because both management and labor have matured to the point where they both see the need for each other, or because other conditions have precipitated the need for participatory management, properly running quality circles are envisioned to become organization norms.

Second, with increasing numbers of companies going out of business, unions are going to have to change their election drive strategies and their images. Our society is clearly moving out of the heavy manufacturing mode, toward service industries. Services have not proved a stronghold area for unions; however, in the mid-1980s, unions are targeting the service sector as a source of potential members. The issues that may make this a fertile area for unionization are not the same issues that existed in heavy manufacturing. As such, union tactics that were once used need to be revised. Some tactics created an image that is not appropriate in the service sector, and that has resulted in many service sector employees frowning on joining unions. This, coupled with the fact that much of this new territory is female, a group not known for its propensity to join unions, is bound to bring about major changes in the job that unions perform and their approaches to recruiting members.

Unions will need to address some of their image problems. More women will need to hold official positions in unions. More important unions are going to have to focus on new concerns of workers. Just hearing what a union *might* be able to do will not be enough for this group. They will need proof. Unions will have to build on appropriate successes to make them more attractive.

If unions are able to break ground in this new territory, new membership should certainly offset losses incurred by plant closings. However, unions must also continue to address the concerns of their loyal past members, for how they help those people will certainly be scrutinized by service industry workers. Catering to and gathering support from these two diverse groups will definitely require a sophisticated balancing capability.

WHERE IS THE LABOR MANAGEMENT RELATIONSHIP GOING?

Throughout this chapter, it has been suggested that both labor and management will be undergoing a lot of changes in the near future. It is important to keep in mind, though, that unions will remain and be a vital part of the labor/management relationship.

While the direction in which to go is known, some organizations will have difficulty implementing these new ideas perfectly and some will even fail to understand the concept at all. Workers will still be mistreated by some, intentionally or unintentionally. Lack of communications, lack of involvement, lack of ways to air complaints, poor working conditions, and low wages will still be found in the marketplace. And unions will remain. They may take on different activities, change some of their images, and represent a new cadre of employees, but they will still take on management for the basic bread and butter issues: wages, hours, terms and conditions of employment, and grievance procedures.

CONCLUSION

Full-circle—the future—smart managers are becoming increasingly aware of the nature of their investments in people. People *are* the best investment. Chosen carefully, maintained thoughtfully, and fueled with adequate wages, fair hours, and a committed concern to nurture their emotional and career-oriented growth needs, the people that make up the labor force will respond better than a well-maintained machine. Labor will produce efficiently, effectively, enthusiastically and will respond with dedication, loyalty, and a commitment to the company and the product.

Bibliography

A. O. Smith Corporation 47LA, 654, 661.

American Federation of Labor. 1939. *Labor and Education.*

American Jurisprudence, 227, pp. 746–748.

American Productivity Center. 1985. *White Collar Productivity Improvement.* Houston, Texas: The American Productivity Center, August.

American Psychological Association. 1985. *Monitor,* Washington, D.C., 16, August, p. 22.

Anderson, Carl R. 1984. *Management: Skills, Functions, and Organization Performance.* Dubuque, Iowa: Wm. C. Brown.

Auerbach, Jerold S. 1966. *Labor and Liberty; the La Follette Committee and the New Deal.* Indianapolis: Bobbs-Merrill, Co.

Bagozzi, Richard. 1975. "Marketing as Exchange." *Journal of Marketing,* 39 (October): pp. 32–39.

Bagozzi, Richard. 1979. "Toward a Formal Theory of Marketing Exchanges." In *Conceptual and Theoretical Developments in Marketing,* edited by Ferrell, Brown, and Lamb. Chicago, Illinois: American Marketing Association, pp. 431–447.

Baldwin, Bruce A. 1985. "Burning Out in America." *Piedmont Airlines,* March, pp. 11–14.

Bank, John and Wilpert Bernhard. 1983. "What's So Special About Quality Circles?" *Journal of General Management,* 9 (Autumn).

Bankston, Eddie. 1976. "Value Differences Between Attorney and Economist Labor Arbitrators." *Industrial Relations Research Association Proceedings of Twenty-Ninth Annual Meeting,* IRRA.

Bartels, Robert. 1974. "The Identity Curve in Marketing." *Journal of Marketing,* 38 (October), pp. 73–76.

Bawen, William G., ed. 1965. *Labor and the National Economy.* New York: W. W. Norton.

Beaty, J. Harold. 1980. *The Rhetoric of Protest and Reform, 1878–1898.* Athens, Ohio: Ohio University.

Beatty, R. S. and C. S. Scheneier. 1981. *Personnel Administration.* 2nd ed. Reading, Massachusetts: Addison-Wesley.

Beinecke, Richard H. 1984. "The Costs of Mental Health and Substance Abuse." *Health Industries of America Report,* January 19, pp. 25–26.

Belcher, D. W. 1974. *Compensation Administration.* Englewood Cliffs, New Jersey: Prentice-Hall.

Bell, C. R. 1977. "Criteria for Selecting Instructional Strategies." *Training and Development Journal* October, 31: 10, pp 3–7.

Berrien, Kenneth. 1968. *General and Social Systems.* New Brunswick, New Jersey: Rutgers University Press.

Blackham, Garth. 1977. *Counseling: Theory, Process, and Practice.* Belmont, California: Wadsworth.

Bright, Thomas, Jerry Weigle, and Stephen Holoviak. 1984. "Employment-At-Will: A Legal Area That Merits Attention for the Small Business Person." *American Journal of Small Business* (Summer): pp. 58–61.

Bureau of Labor Statistics. 1980. *Characteristics of Major Collective Bargaining Agreements, January 1, 1980.* Washington, D.C.: U.S. Bureau of Labor, Bulletin 2095, pp. 83, 92–96.

Bureau of Labor Statistics. 1982. *Productivity Measures for Selected Industries, 1954-80.* Washington, D.C.: U.S. Department of Labor, Bulletin 2128 (April): p. 2.

Bureau of National Affairs. 1983. *Basic Patterns in Union Contracts.* 10th ed. Washington, D.C.: BNA.

Calmer, Alan. 1937. *Labor Agitator, The Story of Albert R. Parsons.* New York: International Publishers.

Carnevale, Anthony Patrick. 1986. "The Learning Enterprise." *Training and Development Journal* (January).

Casey, F. M. *Work Attitudes and Work Experience.* 1979. Washington, D.C.: U.S. Department of Labor, Research and Development Monograph 60.

Casio, Wayne F. 1982. *Costing Human Resources: The Financial Impact of Behavior in Organizations.* Boston, Massachusetts: Kent Publishing, 1982, pp. 45, 60–61.

Collier, B. L. and D. Landen, Jr. 1978. "Industrial Psychology on the Line, Corporate Psychology." *Psychology Today,* 12, pp. 66–67.

"Compensation Currents Benefits." *Compensation Review, American Management Association,* Vol. 11 (First Quarter 1979): p. 10.

Constanzaro, J. L. 1976. "Selecting A Career Path." *Personnel Journal,* 55, pp. 330–31.

Cristiani, T. S. and M. F. Cristiani. 1979. "The Application of Counseling Skills in the Business and Industrial Setting." *The Personnel and Guidance Journal,* 58, pp. 166–69.

Cronon, David E. 1963. *Labor and the New Deal.* Chicago, Illinois: Rand McNally.

DeLeon, David. 1978. *The American as Anarchists: Reflections on Indigenous Radicalism.* Baltimore: Johns Hopkins University Press.

Dewer, Donald. 1980. *The Quality Circle: What You Should Know About It.* California Quality Circle Institute.

Dick, William M. 1972. *Labor and Socialism in America.* Port Washington, New York: Kennikat Press.

Dickson, W. J. and F. Roethlesberger. 1966. *Counseling in an Organization.* Boston, Massachusetts: Harvard University.

Diggins, John P. 1973. *The American Left in the Twentieth Century.* New York: Harcourt Brace Jovanovich. Harbrace History of the U.S., edited by John Morton Blum.

Drucker, Peter F. 1985. "How to Measure White Collar Productivity." *The Wall Street Journal* (November 26).

Elkouri, Frank and Eva Asper Elkouri. 1973. *How Arbitration Works.* 3rd ed. Washington, D.C.: Bureau of National Affairs.

Employee Benefits, 1982. 1983. Washington, D.C.: Chamber of Commerce of the United States.

Employee Involvement Report. Vol. 1, Nos. 1–3. 1985. Oklahoma: Joe Williams Communication.

Eng, J. E. and J. S. Gottsdanker. 1979. "Positive Changes From A Career Development Program." *Training and Development Journal* (January): pp. 3–6.

Engel, James F., Roger D. Blackwell, and Paul W. Minniard. 1986. *Consumer Behavior.* 5th ed. New York: The Dryden Press.

Ewing, D. W. 1981. "Who Wants Corporate Democracy?" *Harvard Business Review* (Spring).

Fairchild, Byron and J. Grossman. 1970. *The Army and Industrial Manpower, the U.S. Army in World War II, The War Department, 1959.* Washington: U.S. Government Printing Office.

Falricant, A. 1981. "The Productivity Issue: An Overview," in *Productivity Prospects for Growth,* edited by J. M. Rosow. New York: D. Van Nostrand.

Feingold, S. N. 1971. *Occupational Counseling in Industry: The Encyclopedia of Education.* New York: MacMillan.

Fiedler, Fred E. and Joseph E. Garcia. 1985. "Comparing Organization Development and Management Training." *Personnel Administrator* (March): p. 36.

Finkelstein, J. T. and J. Ziegenfuss, Jr. 1978. "Diagnosing Employee's Personal Problems." *Personnel Journal,* 57, pp. 634–36.

Fisher, Joann. 1985. "Secretaries Speak Up for Training." *Office Skills Training Report,* McGraw-Hill Training Systems Publication, Issue No. 4 (Spring).

Foner, Philip Sheldon. 1976. *Labor and the American Revolution.* Westport, Connecticut: Greenwood Press.

Fournier, F. F. 1978. *Coaching for Improved Work Performance.* 2nd ed. Englewood Cliffs, New Jersey: Prentice-Hall.

Freeman, Richard L. and James L. Medoff. 1979. "The Two Faces of Unionism." *Public Interest* (Fall): pp. 69–93.

Gable, Myron and Charles Hollon. 1977. *A Survey of Current Retail Practice.* New York: National Retail Merchants Association.

Galenson, Walter. 1959. *Labor and Economic Development.* New York: Wiley.

Gilbert, James Burkhart. 1968. *Writers and Partisans: A History of Literary Radicalism in America.* New York: Wiley.

Gitlow, Abraham L. 1986. *Labor and Industrial Society.* Homewood, Illinois: Irwin.

Glicken, Morely D. 1985. "Don't Let Office Stress Become Your Worst Enemy." *National Business Employment Weekly* (April 28): p. 7.

Gompers, Samuel. 1969. *Labor and the Common Welfare.* New York:

Arna Press. Reprint of 1919 edition.

Gorlin, Harriet and Schein, Lawrence. 1984. *Innovations in Managing Human Resources,* Conference Board Report No. 849. New York: The Conference Board, Inc.

Gould, S. 1978. "Career Planning in the Organization." *Human Resource Management* (Spring): pp. 8–11.

Granof, Michael. 1973. *How to Cost Your Labor Contract.* Washington, D.C.: Bureau of National Affairs.

Gregory, Charles O. 1949. *Labor and the Law,* Second Edition. New York: Norton.

Gutteridge, T. 1980. "Organizational Career Development and Planning." *Readings in Personnel Management: The Utilization of Human Resources,* Edited by H. J. Chruden and W. W. Sherman, 5th ed., Cincinnati, Ohio: South-Western.

Hammer, W. C. and F. J. Smith. 1978. "Work Attitudes as Predicators of Unionization Activity." *Journal of Applied Psychology,* 4, pp. 415–21.

Hampden-Turner, Charles. 1970. *Radical Man: The Process of Psycho-Social Development.* Cambridge, Massachusetts: Schenkman Publishing Company.

Hand, H. H. and J. W. Solcum. 1972. "A Longitudinal Study of the Effects of Human Relations Training on Managerial Effectiveness," *Journal of Applied Psychology,* 56, pp. 412–17.

Hautaluoma, J. E. and J. F. Gavin. 1975. "Effects of Organizational Diagnosis and Intervention on Blue Collar Blues." *Journal of Applied Behavior Science,* 11, pp. 475–596.

Hays, Paul Raymond. 1966. *Labor Arbitration: A Dissenting View.* New Haven: Yale University Press.

Heisel, W. D. and Gordon S. Skinner. 1976. *Costing Union Demands.* Milwaukee: Public Employees Relations Library.

Helfgott, Roy B. 1980. *Labor Economics,* 2nd ed. New York: Random House.

Henderson, Richard I. 1985. *Compensation Management and Rewarding Performance,* 4th ed. Reston Publishing Company.

Henle, Peter. 1973. "Reverse Collective Bargaining: A Look at Some Union Concession Situations." *Industrial and Labor Relations Review,* Vol. 26 (April): p. 565.

Hodgskin, Thomas. 1969. *Labor Defended Against the Claims of Capital; or The Unproductiveness of Capital Proved with Reference to the Present Combinations Amongst Journeymen.* New York: A. M. Kelley.

Hofstadter, Richard. 1959. *Social Darwinism in American Thought.* New York: G. Braziller.

Holly, William and Kenneth Jennings. 1984. *The Labor Relations Process.* New York: Dryden Press.

Holoviak, Stephen J. 1984. *Costing Labor Contracts and Judging Their Financial Impact.* New York: Praeger.

Holoviak, Stephen J. 1984. "Career Planning — A Link to Better Productivity." *Performance and Instruction Journal,* 23: 7, October, pp. 7–8.

Holoviak, Stephen J. 1982. "The Impact of Training on Company Productivity Levels." *Performance and Instruction Journal,* 21: 5, June, pp. 6–8.

Holoviak, Stephen J., David A. Decenzo, and Sharon Brookens Holoviak. 1985. "Assess the Needs for Counseling Education Among Industrial Personnel." *Performance and Instruction,* Vol. 24, April, pp. 1–5.

Holoviak, Stephen J. and Sharon Brookens Holoviak. 1984. "The Benefits of In-House Counseling." *Personnel,* 61: 4, July-August, pp. 53–59.

Huberman, John. 1964. "Discipline, Not Punishment." *Harvard BusiReview* (July-August): pp. 62–68.

Hunt, Shelby D. 1976. *Marketing Theory: Conceptual Foundations of Research in Marketing.* Colombus, Ohio: Grid, Inc.

Jaffe, Julian F. 1972. *Crusade Against Radicalism.* Port Washington, New York: National University Publications.

Jennings, Ken and Roger Walters. 1976. "Discharge Cases Recommended." *Arbitration Journal,* 31 (September): pp. 164–84.

Jones, Edgar A., Jr. 1966. "Problems of Proof in the Arbitration Process: Report of West Coast Tripartite Committee." *Problems of Proof in Arbitration: Proceedings of the Nineteenth Annual Meeting,* National Academy of Arbitrators. Washington, D.C.: BNA.

Kastelanetz, Richard. 1968. *Beyond Left and Right: Radical Thought for Our Times.* New York: Morrow.

Kerr, Clark. 1964. *Labor and Management in Industrial Society.* Garden City, New York: Anchor Books.

Kirby, Paula and S. J. Holoviak. 1985. "Evaluating Quality Circle Programs." *1985 International Quality Circle Annual Conference Transactions,* Cincinnati, Ohio, IAQC (April): pp. 157–60.

Kochan, Thomas. 1980. *Collective Bargaining and Industrial Relations.* Homewood, Illinois: Richard D. Irwin.

Kraditor, Aileen S. 1981. *The Radical Persuasion 1890–1917.* Baton Rouge: Louisiana State University.

LaGreca, Genevieve. 1985. "The Stress You Make." *Personnel Journal* (September): p. 43.

Larson, Simeon. 1975. *Labor and Foreign Policy.* London: Farleigh Dickinson Press.

Laslett, John. 1970. *Labor and the Left: A Study of Socialist and Radical Influences in the American Labor Movement, 1881–1924.* New York: Basic Books.

Lauer, Jeanne and D. G. Patterson. 1951. "Readability of Union Contracts." *Personnel,* 28: 1, pp. 36–40.

Leonard, N. M. 1977. "The Counseling Psychologists as an Organizational Consultant." *The Counseling Psychologist,* 1, p. 3.

Levy, Sidney J. 1959. "Symbols for Sale." *Harvard Business Review,*

37 (July-August): pp. 117–19.

Lewis, H. Gregg. 1963. *Unionism and Relative Wages in the United States.* Chicago: University of Chicago Press.

List, Charles E. 1982. "How to Make Quality Circles Work for Your Organization." *Personnel Journal* (September): pp. 652–54.

Lusterman, Seymour. 1985. *Trends in Corporate Education and Training,* Conference Board Report No. 870. New York: The Conference Board, Inc.

Lynd, Staughton (ed). 1973. *American Labor Realism: Testimonies and Interpretations.* New York: Wiley.

Lynd, Staughton. 1968. *Intellectual Origins of American Radicalism.* New York: Pantheon Books.

Maguire, John MacArthur. 1947. *Evidence: Common Sense and Common Law.* Oneda, New York: Foundation Press.

Maher, John Edward. 1965. *Labor and the Economy.* Boston: Allyn and Bacon.

Marcuse, Herbert. 1972. *Counterrevolution and Revolt.* Boston: Beacon Press.

McCarthy, E. Jerome and William D. Perreault, Jr. 1984. *Basic Marketing: A Managerial Approach.* 8th ed. Homewood, Illinois: Richard D. Irwin, Inc.

Milbourn, Gene, Jr. 1984. "Alcoholism, Drug Abuse, Job Stress: What Small Business Can Do." *American Journal of Small Business,* 8 (April-June): pp. 36–48.

Miles, J. B. 1985. "How to Help Troubled Workers." *Computer Decisions,* 17 (February): pp. 66–67.

Miller, S. M. and M. Kroll. 1970. "Strategies for Reducing Credentialism," *Good Government,* Summer, pp. 10–13.

Miller, Sally M. 1974. *The Radical Immigrant.* New York: Twayne Publishers.

Modecraft Company, 44 LA 1045, 1049.

Moore, Gary and Randyl Elkin. 1983. *Labor and Economy.* Cincinnati, Ohio: Southwestern.

Moore, Wilbert Ellis, and Feldman, Arnold S. 1960. *Labor Commitment and Social Change in Developing Areas.* New York: Social Science Research Council.

Mroczkowski, Tomasz. 1984. "Quality Circles, Fine—What Next?" *Personnel Administrator,* June.

Nellis, David. 1984. "Starting and Developing Quality Circles." *1985 IAQC Annual Conference Transactions,* Cincinnati, Ohio, IAQC (April): pp. 337–39.

New York Stock Exchange, Office of Economic Research. 1982. *People and Productivity: A Challenge to Corporate America.* New York.

New York Times. 1985. "Japanese Companies in the U.S. Seen Excelling," March 18.

Niehouse, Olivia L. 1984. "Measuring Your Burnout Potential." *Supervising Management* (July): pp. 29–31.

Odione, George S. 1985. "Human Resource Strategies for the '80s." *Training* (January): p. 49.

Oswald, Rudy. 1981. "Unions and Productivity." *Productivity: Pros-*

pects for Growth, edited by Jerome M. Rosow, pp. 98–99. New York: D. Van Nostrand.

"Personnel's Newest Source, Counseling." 1978. *Personnel Administrator,* 23, pp. 37–38.

Piehl, Mel. 1982. *Breaking Bread: The Catholic Worker and the Origin of Catholic Radicalism in America.* Philadelphia: Temple University Press.

Prasow, Paul and Edward Peters. 1983. *Arbitration and Collective Bargaining: Conflict Resolution in Labor Relations.* 2nd. ed. New York: McGraw-Hill.

Raphael, M. A. 1975. "Work Preview Can Reduce Turnover and Improve Performance." *Personnel Journal,* 54, pp. 97–98.

Rees, Albert. 1959. "Patterns of Wages, Prices and Productivity," *Wages, Prices, Profits, and Productivity.* New York: American Assembly.

Richardson, Peter R. 1985. "Courting Greater Employee Involvement Through Participative Management." *Sloan Management Review,* Winter.

Robins, J. 1979. "Costly Problems: Firms Try Newer Ways to Slash Absenteeism as Carrot and Stick Fail." *Wall Street Journal,* March 14, p. 35.

Rosow, J. M. 1979. "Quality of Work-life Issues in the 1980s," in *Work in American the Decade Ahead,* edited by C. Kerr and J. M. Rosow. New York: D. Van Nostrand.

Rostain, H. 1980. "New York City's Approach to Problem—Employee Counseling." *Personnel Journal,* 59, pp. 309–21.

Scheifer, Victor J. 1979. "Cost of Living Adjustment: Keeping Up with Inflation." *Monthly Labor Review* (June): pp. 14–16.

Schein, E. H. 1971. "The Individual, the Organization, and the Career: A Conceptual Scheme." *Journal of Applied Behavioral Science,* 7, pp. 401–426.

Schuster, Frederick. 1985. *Human Resources Management: Concepts, Cares, and Readings.* 2nd. ed. Reston, Virginia: Reston Publishing.

Seidman, Harold. 1938. *Labor Czars: A History of Labor Racketeering.* New York: Leveright Publishing Corporation.

Shaw, Marvin E. and Philip R. Costanzo. 1982. *Theories of Social Psychology.* 2nd. ed. New York: McGraw-Hill.

Sheth, Jagdish N. and David M. Gardner. 1982. "History of Marketing Thought: An Update." In *Marketing Theory: Philosophy of Science Perspectives,* edited by Ronald Bush and Shelby Hunt. Chicago, Illinois: American Marketing Association, pp. 52–58.

Siegel, Boaz. 1965. *Proving Your Arbitration Case.* Washington, D.C.: BNA.

Sirgy, M. Joseph. 1984. *Marketing As Social Behavior: A General Systems Theory.* New York: Praeger.

Sovereign, Kenneth. 1984. *Personnel Law.* Reston, Virginia: Reston Publishing.

Sperry Corporation. *Quality Circle Training Program: Facilitator Manual.* Princeton, New Jersey, 1983.

Sutcliff, Jon and Jay Schuster. 1985. "Benefits Revisited, Benefits Predicted." *Personnel Journal* (September): p. 62.

Stessin, Lawrence. 1960. *Employee Discipline.* Washington, D.C.: BNA. 2–3.

Suchan, James and Clyde Scott. 1984. "Readability Levels of Collective Bargaining Agreements." *Personnel Administrator,* 29: 11, November, pp. 73–80.

Thornton, G. C., III. 1978. "Differential Effects of Career Planning on Intervals and Externals." *Personnel Psychology,* 31, p. 471.

Tiffin, Joseph and Francis Walsh. 1951. "Readability of Union Management Agreements." *Personnel Psychology,* 4: 4, pp. 327–38.

Trotta, Maurice. 1976. *Handling Grievances: A Guide for Management and Labor.* Washington, D.C.: BNA.

U.S. Coal Development, Promises and Uncertainties, 1977, Washington, D.C. Report to Congress, 1977 of Comptroller General, pp. 4.6 to 4.57.

U.S. Department of Labor, Bureau of Labor-Management Relations and Cooperative Programs. 1984. *Labor-Management Cooperation: Perspectives from the Labor Movement,* Washington, D.C.

Wald, Alan M. 1983. *The Revolutionary Imagination: The Poetry and Politics of John Wheelwright and Sherry Mangan.* Chapel Hill: University of North Carolina Press.

Walker, J. W. 1976. "Let's Get Realistic About Career Paths," *Human Resource Management,* 15, pp. 2–7.

Walker, S. C. 1981. "The Dynamics of Clear Contract Language." *Personnel Journal,* 60: 1, pp. 39–41.

Wechsler, James Arthur. 1972. *Labor Baron: A Portrait of John L. Lewis.* Westport, Connecticut: Greenwood Press.

Wellington, Harry H. 1968. *Labor and the Legal Process.* New Haven: Yale University Press.

Wheeler, Hoyt N. 1976. "Punishment Theory in Industrial Discipline." *Industrial Relations,* 15: 2, May, pp. 235–43.

Wilkie, William L. 1986. *Consumer Behavior.* New York: John Wiley and Sons.

Wright, Peter and David Taylor. 1984. *Improving Leadership Performance.* Englewood Cliffs, New Jersey: Prentice Hall Inc.

Yelowitz, Irwin. 1965. *Labor and the Progressive Movement in New York State, 1897–1916.* Ithaca: Cornell University Press.

Young, Alfred F. (ed). 1968. *Dissent.* DeKalb: Northern Illinois University Press.

Zalusky, John. 1976. "Arbitration: Updating a Vital Process." *American Federationist* (November): pp. 1–8.

Index

About the Authors

Stephen J. Holoviak is Professor of Labor Relations at Shippensburg University of Pennsylvania. In addition, he is Director of the Harry Rankin Frehn Center for Management at the University. Prior to his teaching career, he spent ten years in private industry as a financial executive.

Dr. Holoviak has published widely in the area of labor relations, compensation, and participative management. His first book, *Costing Labor Contracts and Judging Their Financial Impact,* was published in 1984 by Praeger Publishers. He has written articles in *Compensation and Benefits Review, Personnel, Akron Business and Economic Review, Performance and Instruction Journal,* and the *American Journal of Small Business.* Dr. Holoviak is also an active consultant in the area of labor relations, compensation administration, and is an arbitrator and mediator.

Dr. Holoviak holds the B.S.B.A. from Henderson State University, the M.S.M. from Frostburg State College, and the M.A. and Ph.D. from West Virginia University, Morgantown, West Virginia.

Susan Stone Sipkoff is Assistant Professor of Marketing at Shippensburg University of Pennsylvania. In addition, she is a doctoral student at The George Washington University in Washington, D.C.

Professor Sipkoff taught regularly on a part-time basis for The Pennsylvania State University, Wilson College, and Shippensburg prior to accepting a full-time position with Shippensburg University. During that time, she also worked in industry as Director of Marketing for VSP Wastewater Technology and as an independent consultant in management and marketing.

Professor Sipkoff has presented papers to the American Collegiate Retailing Association and the Academy of Marketing Science. "The Effect of Demographic Variables on Energy Use in a Developing Country" by Sipkoff and Lynn Harris was published in the 1985 *Academy of Marketing Science Conference Proceedings.*

Professor Sipkoff holds the A.B. from Wilson College and the M.B.A. from Shippensburg University.